The Letter

The Letter

SARAH SIDEBOTTOM
WITH SUNDAY TIMES BESTSELLING AUTHOR
ANN CUSACK

mB
MIRROR BOOKS

m
B

MIRROR BOOKS

1

Published in Great Britain and Ireland in 2024 by
Mirror Books, a Reach PLC business.

Photographic Acknowledgements: Alamy

www.mirrorbooks.co.uk
@TheMirrorBooks

Print ISBN 9781915306807
eBook ISBN 9781915306814

Editor: Jo Sollis
Cover Design: Jonah Webb

Printed and bound in Great Britain by
CPI Group (UK) Ltd, Croydon, CR0 4YY

MIX
Paper | Supporting
responsible forestry
FSC
www.fsc.org
FSC® C171272

I would like to thank my husband Darren who has walked every step of this journey with me towards justice and been supportive of me in writing this book.

Thank for the emotional support you have given me throughout the bad times, the dark times and happy times.

I will be forever grateful, and I will love you always and look forward to a happier future together. We got through this, we can get through anything.

Prologue

"HAVE YOU seen this letter?" gasped my husband, Darren. "Sarah? You need to look at this, love. Now."

He waved a freshly printed sheet of paper under my nose, just as I was taking a sip of my coffee.

"You need to look at this," he insisted again, his voice urgent, fearful.

Instinctively, I shrank back, as though the paper itself might be infected. In that small sliver of a moment, I was plunged right back to the horror of my childhood. That same fear bloomed in my chest now, just as it had then. Why?

"What is it?" I asked quietly.

He laid the letter on the table in front of me and didn't speak. Gulping in air, I scanned the first three lines, and my heart clenched in disbelief. It was as though my head was being forced under icy cold water. Every time I came up for oxygen, I was ducked back under. My coffee cup fell to the floor, scalding my knees, splashing the rug, but I barely noticed. I saw again those blue bedroom walls. I felt his wet breath rasping in my ear. His beard scratching my cheek.

The Letter

But mostly, I remembered the hand. I could never forget that hand. The pudgy fingers; a smell like raw liver. The big meaty palm, clamped over my mouth. My eyes wide in terror, pleading mutely to be spared.

"You tell anyone, I'll shoot you."

I was three and half years old. A mere wisp of a little girl, the innocence shining out of me like sunlight. Physically, mentally, he had torn me apart. Pitched me into a darkness from which I would never escape.

"Sarah?" Darren said, his hand on mine. "Are you OK? Have you read it? Do you know what this means?"

Tears which I had had held in for five decades now streamed down my cheeks; rivers of grief. The shock of seeing my injuries in black and white, the brutal confirmation of my suffering, was like a razorblade right across my soul. I knew immediately that this was likely to be the vital piece in a prosecution jigsaw puzzle. This letter was my written witness. My key to justice. Inside this hellish wrapping nestled a glittering golden nugget. But why the cover-up? Why had nobody told me? I had grown up on the wrong side of a wall of silence. My own mother, the one person I should have been able to trust, had lied to me my whole life. Or at least, she had avoided the truth. And yet the betrayal was strangely galvanising.

I read the letter again, retching at the graphic details, but with a fight stirring deep inside. Hope fluttered up from the page and into the air. I was determined to see this through. Yes, this was an atom bomb. But it was also the key to a justice I had dreamed of for almost 50 years.

Chapter One

MARSHMALLOW CLOUDS scudded across a blue sky and the sunshine was warm and welcoming. Perfect weather for a paddle.

"Come on! Into the pool!" I called, tucking my dress up and kicking off my sandals.

My older brother, Stephen, aged six, scampered after me to the bottom of the garden to our family 'swimming pool'. The pool was, in fact, an old man-made well, leftover from one of my dad's building projects. It was filled with rainwater and though it was deep in the middle we could climb over the low stone surround, and paddle around the edges. Nowadays, it would doubtless be a health and safety hazard but back then, in the summer of 1973, we thought it was the height of luxury.

"No splashing," I giggled, as I dipped in a toe.

We spent the next few hours jumping in and out, squealing dramatically when the water lapped over our clothes, teeth chattering when the sun went behind a cloud. Later, inside the house, we dried off and got into our pyjamas. Stephen helped me to find my slippers and held my hand to steady me as I walked back downstairs. Our mum, Florence, had already left for work at the local pub and had prepared homemade meat pie and mash, ready to reheat in the oven. Our father, Arthur William Bowditch, known as Bill, never cooked. Stephen and I ate at the kitchen table, feeding the scraps to our little dog, Puff, a brown and white mixed breed.

"She loves pie," I beamed, as Puff lay down, under my chair.

To the outsider, it was a tableau of domestic bliss. And to the lady in the local shop, to the postman, the milkman, the vicar, we must have seemed like a normal, happy, family. Comfortably well off, we lived in a three-bedroomed detached house, built of light-brown bricks, with a traditional glass front door. Downstairs was a large living room, kitchen-dining room, and a small office for my father. We wore hand-me-downs and jumble sale clothes, but then, so did many of our friends. We didn't have many toys or luxuries, but again, it was the same for lots of other children.

Arthur Stephen, known as just Stephen, was the eldest and I was aged four. We were warm and well-fed, well-behaved and polite, and there was nothing to mark us out from any other family. Mum, as was typical of the era, was the main caregiver. But she was often ill; she had breathing problems from a spell of whooping cough as a child and was in and out of hospital throughout her life. When she was well, she worked as a chef, and did all of our cooking and cleaning, on top of the childcare. Dad was a builder, a stocky man, strong and solid, though not especially tall, with a beard and dark brown eyes. He had a rich Somerset accent, and a loud voice. He was strict, with a rigid set of regulations, for his children and his wife. An old-fashioned disciplinarian, he was, to the outsider, quite typical of his generation:

"Children should be seen and not heard."

"Make your bed each morning."No shoes allowed in the house."

Our home was clinically clean and tidy, though I was never sure if Mum was naturally houseproud or whether she was simply adhering to Dad's rules. If we stepped out of line, we got a slap, or even a whack with his brown leather belt. I remember even now the stomach-churning anticipation of holding out my hands, fingers trembling, eyes screwed shut, as the belt thwacked down towards my hands. Yet many parents were like that, back in the 1970s. It wasn't unusual to get a smack for bad behaviour or bad manners. He and Mum had fierce rows too, which often ended with Dad's fists flying. It tugged at my heartstrings, watching her plaster heavy make-up over a black eye or a split lip before she went to work. I didn't understand why she took such care to cover her injuries, and why, the more make-up she wore, the sadder she seemed. Dad's violence was never discussed or referenced in any way, by Mum, by us, or by anyone. But again, attitudes to domestic abuse were very different back then.

"You make your bed, you lie in it," was one of Mum's sayings, and she seemed to live by that. She just got on with her day and put up with Dad the way he was. And in the village, he was well known and well-liked. He was popular and chatty and always happy to put himself out for people.

The Letter

He might be called upon out of hours if a neighbour's roof rained in or a garden wall collapsed. He'd turn up, with his tool belt and a ready smile.

"What would we do without your Dad?" the neighbours would say, and I would bob my head in confusion, for I thought I'd do very well without him, thank you. My view, as a four-year old, was that he was good with bricks, not so good with people. Lying in bed, I'd hear his voice booming out around the house. He had a big personality. A big voice. And so people presumed he had a big heart, too.

But there were fragments of memory, sharp as shards of glass, which rose to the surface, sometimes in my daydreams, other times in my sleep. The meaty hand clamped across my mouth. The agony ripping my small body apart. The tendrils of pain reaching right up through my stomach. The stale smell of cigars. The scratchy beard. The blue bedroom walls. My mother standing at the bottom of the stairs, her face bleached of colour. Raised voices in the hallway. The blood, warm and sticky, between my legs.

If anyone asks, you fell down the stairs. Not long after it happened, my brother pinched our mother's nail polish and painted red rivers down those same blue walls. It became a chapter in our family folklore. *Remember the mess he made of the walls!* But I could not see those red lines without remembering the meaty hand, the screams, and the dark red blood which congealed in my underwear.

* * * *

There was a great commotion in our house when, before my sixth birthday, Mum announced we would be moving to a village called Alford, in Somerset. Dad planned to build our next house all by himself, and we would live in two caravans until it was ready.

"Caravans!" I shrieked, my enthusiasm bubbling over as I danced around the living room.

As a little girl, I couldn't imagine anything more exciting. Living in a caravan seemed like the next best thing to a permanent holiday, and I'd never actually been on holiday in my life.

Arriving at the site itself we found a huge mud-bath with piles of bricks, stones and sand dotted around. In one corner, two old fashioned touring caravans were parked side by side, so it was possible to hop from one to the other. The first caravan was our living area, the second was for sleeping. Mum and Dad slept at one end of the caravan on a pull-out bed, with me and my brother at the other end. Mum's health was up and down as always. She'd had lung surgery when I was a baby, but never really seemed well. Mum's health problems became a real struggle, and she often became tired and weak, and too ill to care for us properly. The novelty of living in the caravans faded faster than anticipated too; it was cramped and chaotic and tempers were frayed. There was mud and packing boxes everywhere; it was impossible to find the right item of clothing or that one missing shoe. We were living in such a muddle. One evening, still in his work boots, Dad poked his head round the door of the caravan and said, with a slight incline of his head:

The Letter

"Sarah, go and get ready for bed." My father was not usually involved in childcare and certainly didn't tuck us into bed. But I did as I was told, hurrying into the second caravan and changing into a white, flowery nightie, which I didn't like at all, because it was polyester and itched against my skin. I was gathering my clothes for the laundry when the bedroom door opened, and Dad walked in. His bulk, against the flimsy caravan walls and the low ceiling, seemed somehow sinister and threatening. He looked too big and broad for the poky little bedroom. I had a brief, strange thought that he could push the walls out with his bare hands and collapse the lot on top of us."Lie back on the bed," he ordered.

Dropping my laundry, I perched on the end of the bed, suddenly nervous. There was a charge in the room, an anxiety. I felt even the caravan walls were bending slightly under the pressure. Dad put one hand on my chest and shoved me, so that I was flat on my back on the bed. My little legs dangled over the edge; I wasn't yet tall enough for my feet to touch the floor. He undid his belt, the buckle clinking softly as his trousers dropped to his knees. He pushed my nightie up, I wasn't allowed to wear underwear in bed, it was one of the rules, so I was naked from the waist down. Out of his pocket, he took a Nivea tub, which I recognised as Mum's moisturiser. He wiped a dollop onto his finger before reaching down between my legs and pushing it inside me.

The shock took my breath away.

And the discomfort, a scratchy, rough sort of pain, brought tears to my eyes. I wondered briefly whether he'd grown his fingernails long. Now I know it was probably the rough skin on his hands which felt so abrasive in such a sensitive area. He masturbated, faster and faster, and it was as mesmerising as it was gut-wrenching. Aged six, I had no idea what he was doing. Neither did I link it with the flashbacks from the blue bedroom. Abruptly, Dad withdrew his finger, yanked me out of the way, and ejaculated, leaving a wet patch on my bed.

"This is our secret, me and you," he hissed, making no real effort to keep his voice down. "If you ever tell anyone, they won't believe you and you will have to go back into care. Nobody will like you and nobody will visit you.

"And −" he half-smiled, as though this was an amusing afterthought − "I might kill your mother whilst you're gone."

I shrank back on the bed, petrified. I had never been so scared. His words were spine-chilling. Worse, these were not empty threats, plucked at random from his imagination. I knew I had been in the care system, as a toddler. And I was also aware that Dad kept guns; he made no secret of it. So it seemed possible, probable even, that he would and could carry out everything he had promised.

My small heart hammered against my ribs as he stalked out of the bedroom and out of the caravan. I was frightened by what he had said, confused by what had happened, and completely overwhelmed. Unable to think it all through or even allow myself to be upset, instead, my mind became a blank nothing. After I'd put my clothes into the laundry basket, I climbed into bed, taking care to avoid the damp stain, and forced myself to float away into the nothingness.

Chapter Two

BECAUSE OF Mum's deteriorating health, it was decided I should be packed off to stay with my maternal Nan, Grace, who lived in a pretty seaside village called Aberaeron in South Wales. Visiting Nan was always a huge treat. Her house was a four-hour car journey away, and we livened it up by playing 'I spy'. There was invariably a clamour to be the first to spot the imposing Severn Bridge in the distance, and to see a pink castle which nestled in the trees at the side of the road.

"I saw it first! I saw it first!" Stephen yelled.

"Not fair!" I whined. "I can't see. I'm not big enough."

Nan was plump, with a round, smiley face, and grey hair with a slight wave in it. Every morning she would put red and blue rollers in her hair and wrap one of her many coloured scarves over the top. Nan always had a warm welcome waiting. I adored her. And the best of it was, she adored me too.

"Come here," she beamed, wrapping her arms around me as I raced up the path towards her.

I didn't get affection at home. There were no cuddles, no kisses. Dad was too angry and authoritarian, and Mum was too harassed and busy, always preoccupied with her own troubles, with not enough time to bother about mine. I was raised on a diet of strict restraint, and no matter how much I longed for that cuddle, my mother never cracked, not even for a moment. She seemed distant, never really fully present, as though there was a screen between us. Sometimes I wanted to tap on the glass and shout: "Mum! Please listen to me!"

Nan was everything my mother wasn't – tactile, loving and gentle. With her arms around me, I drank her in; the scent of her favourite Lily of The Valley talcum powder, mixed with cooking smells. She always wore a brooch pinned to her cardigan, and I was entranced by the way the little jewels shone, just as she did. As a small girl, I imagined the jewels were valuable, and that Nan must have regal importance, just like the Queen. Certainly, she was my Queen.

"You're going to be staying here a while this time," she told me that first night, as she smoothed the blankets. "So you'll be going to the local school, OK?"

Wide-eyed, I nodded. The news was getting better and better. I had a fleeting thought that perhaps I might never have to go home at all. And, as I had hoped and anticipated, it was bliss living with Nan. When we weren't out shopping, or walking, she taught me to bake Welsh cakes, and Cawl, her speciality Welsh stew. I'd stand alongside her, on a kitchen chair, peeling potatoes and carrots whilst she sliced the lamb.

"We're a smashing team, you and me," she smiled.

The Letter

In the evenings, she and I would snuggle up on her sofa and watch *Coronation Street* and *Emmerdale Farm*. She loved all the soaps, and together we would follow the plotlines diligently. At suppertime, she'd make me tea and toast, before tucking me into bed. It was so unusual to be nurtured and fussed over like this. Nan made me feel special; I had no doubt how much I was loved and valued by her.

In keeping with everything connected to Nan, the local school was lovely too. I settled in and made friends easily. Nan worked as a cleaner at the nearby comprehensive school and my grandad, John, was a caretaker, so the local community felt like distant family members.

One day, in class, my teacher asked me to stand up and recite the six times table. Maths was not my strong point, but I did well until I reached 6x9, and then I faltered. There was an awkward silence, during which I felt myself flushing redder and redder. As luck would have it, another teacher was walking through the classroom, bringing in new books, and as he passed my chair, he whispered, "54" and winked at me. I beamed, said my answer out loud, and sat down in relief. I loved it here, in Aberaeron, where the sea air filled my lungs with new energy, and everything just seemed to fall into place.

After the final school bell, Nan would be waiting in the playground. Whilst she brushed and mopped classroom floors, I lifted chairs onto tables, or took the bins outside. After her work was done, we'd have a snack at home, a jam butty perhaps, before I started my homework. Nan was quite strict about my homework, and it had to be finished before I was allowed to play outside.

In winter, we stayed in, watching TV; *Blue Peter, Play Away* and all the soaps. In summer, we went to the park or to the beach. There was a river nearby, with lots of walkways, too. Nan had her own routine, just as we had at home. What I did not understand, aged six, was why Nan's routine was pleasant and reassuring, and offered a welcome structure to the day. And yet my parents' routine at home was oppressive and stifling. My mother, brittle and tightly coiled, was like a stranger to me. Nan, in contrast, was open and unfolded, like the pages of a favourite book. What was so wrong with my home life that I felt suffocated just living there? How could two routines be so diametrically different? At Christmas, we performed a concert and I had to learn a song in Welsh. I couldn't speak a word, and I was terrified.

"Just open and close your mouth," Nan suggested. "Nobody will be any the wiser."

I did as she said, and it seemed to work well. Nobody noticed, except Nan of course, who gave me a wink as she clapped and cheered in the audience. I loved the idea that she and I shared a secret.

At weekends, the pop man would visit Nan's, dropping off bottles of lemonade and cream soda. I collected bottle tops and empty glass bottles, to return to the local shop for a penny or two in return. Nan's corner shop was called: 'Mr Grimley's' and he had an array of penny sweets on display; Fruit Salads, Black Jacks, gobstoppers and Refreshers. It took me ages to choose 10 sweets: the act of choosing them was almost more mouth-wateringly delicious than the sweets themselves! The funny thing was, when Mr Grimley handed me my 10p paper bag of goodies, he'd pass me back my 10p too.

"Off you go," he grinned, with a wink.

I didn't understand it then, but looking back, I wonder whether he saw in me a tinge of sadness, deprivation, or trauma. It was a small kindness, but it has stuck with me throughout my life. I wish I could tell him now how I appreciated those good deeds.

On Tuesday evenings, Nan and Grandad took me to a whist drive at the local British Legion. Nan and Grandad were presidents of the British Legion and very proud of their roles. When Autumn came around, large sheets of flat poppies arrived at the house, and I was allowed to help Grandad pop them out, and plump the petals, ready for sale. He and I wrapped up in scarves and gloves, him in his customary flat cap, me in a woolly bobble hat, and we went out in the wind and rain, selling poppies around the town. And though I was not allowed to actually make a sale, because I was too young, Grandad said I was his best asset.

"We've sold three times as many poppies today," he smiled. "That's all thanks to you, Sarah."

One afternoon, on our way home, we spotted a poster advertising filming for *Play Away* in the local community hall.

"Can I go, Nan?" I asked. "I could be on telly."

"Course you can," she replied, as I relayed the details. "I'm looking forward to having a celebrity in the family!"

I went along that weekend and queued to be in the TV audience. Later in the year, there was a fleeting glimpse of my excited face on children's TV.

"See," Nan said proudly. "I said you'd be famous, and you are!"

She enrolled me at Brownies too, and I borrowed a uniform which had belonged to one of my aunts. I joined the Gnomes and enthusiastically set about collecting all the art and craft badges, which were my favourites, and which Nan sewed onto my sleeve. Like a small flower, starved of water and light, I was being coaxed into the warmth, and slowly beginning to thrive and blossom.

"I am so proud of you," Nan told me.

I smiled and deep down I hoped that one day I could be proud of myself, too.

* * * *

I had been living at Nan's a few months when Mum and Dad visited.

"We've come to take you home," Mum announced, and I felt suddenly punctured, the happiness hissing out of me.

I didn't want to leave Nan. Not yet. Not ever. I was safe there, more at home than I could ever be with my own parents. Mum must have noticed my disappointment and I imagine she was hurt or even jealous; my bond with Nan brought into sharp focus our own fractured and remote relationship. Today, just as any other time when she collected me from Nan's, she quickly became ratty and short-tempered as I tried, in vain, to delay our departure.

"Just get into the car,. No, I don't want to try your Welsh cakes, we haven't got time, not today."

The Letter

That night, back in my caravan bed, I wished I could go and live with Nan forever. Her house was like a little slice of sunlight in my dark world.

In April 1976, I was back at Nan's for my 7th birthday. To my amazement, she announced she was planning a party for me. I'd never had a party before. My birthday was usually marked with a small gift from my parents, nothing more. I collected Whimsies, a series of miniature animal figures, and so usually I asked for one or two of those. But today, Nan had other ideas.

"Let's celebrate," she beamed, already busy buttering bread for buffet sandwiches.

"A party?" I asked incredulously. "For me?"

Nan invited a few of her neighbours and a couple of the kids I'd been at school with the previous year. My aunt had recently got married and Nan had bagged the top tier of her wedding cake for my birthday cake. She stuck seven candles into the white icing, and I swelled with excitement. I'd never blown candles out in my life.

"Make a wish!" Nan said as she struck a match. "Have a good think."

As everyone gathered around the table, I closed my eyes and made out as if I was thinking hard. But I already knew. There was no contest. No deliberation. My wish was simple; to live with Nan for the rest of my life.

"Done it!" I announced, opening my eyes.

I truly believed, as I blew out my candles, that my wish would come true. Perhaps it would be instant, and I could move in here and now, and never have to go home ever again.

Would my clothes appear here, in the wardrobe at Nan's, by magic? Would my Whimsies fly cross-country, over the Severn Bridge, landing in Aberaeron? Even if they didn't, I wasn't fussed. I could live without the lot, as long as I had Nan. All afternoon, we played party games, Musical Bumps and Pass the Parcel. Nan had made jam butties and she handed out jelly and ice cream, and birthday cake wrapped in napkins. I got a doll too; my first ever brand-new dolly. I was so happy; it was almost like a dream, an enchanted journey. When, that evening, Mum handed me my coat and said:

"Time to get going," I felt my heart stutter.

What about my birthday wish? I wanted to shout. *Why can't I live here forever?*

But Mum was already steering me towards the door, muttering under her breath. The journey home was silent. We passed the pink castle, and I felt a surge of resentment. As we pulled into our driveway, the last dregs of birthday exuberance leaked out like the air from one of my party balloons.

"Shoes!" bawled my father, as Mum and I stepped in through the front door.

Like frightened rabbits, we both removed our footwear and stepped into the hallway in our socks. Dad, glowering at us from the living room doorway, was wearing his work boots. The house rules, made by him, did not apply to him. Even as a little girl, I could see the injustice, but I was too afraid, and too wise, to mention it.

"Straight to bed," my father said, and I scurried gratefully up the stairs, with my new doll under my arm. Looking out

The Letter

of my bedroom window, at the half-moon and the stars, I wondered if Nan could see them too. Her home, and everything in it, already seemed like an illusion, a temporary fancy, a mythical oasis. There could not have been a greater contrast between the warmth and love at Nan's and the cruel, twisted, regime at my home. Nan's was four hours away, but life was so different there, she might as well have been on another planet, or the most distant star. How foolish I had been to think I could ever have deserved a share of such happiness. For me, birthday wishes did not come true.

Chapter Three

WE LIVED in the caravans for almost two years whilst the building work continued at a slow pace. Mum's health was unpredictable, and she was in and out of hospital for short periods. Dad didn't ever look after us on his own; he was a workaholic, out seven days a week. But even if he'd been unemployed, he wouldn't have agreed to look after his children; that just wasn't his thing.

Sometimes, an aunt would come to help out. Or, if it was for longer than a few days, I'd go to stay with Nan. I was used to this domestic upheaval and actually, I looked forward to it. It seemed it had been going on since before my memories were made, as Mum had told me I'd been in foster care, several times during 1971, when I was just two years old.

"I wasn't well enough to look after you," she said. "So you had to go to another family."

Even as a seven-year-old, the revelation stung. I'd been separated from everything I knew, plonked into a strange family, without a single familiar face around me.

"Why couldn't someone else look after me?" I asked Mum. "And where were you? Were you in hospital?"

But Mum had no more to say. Before I'd finished my question, she had already pulled back and drawn down the shutters. Her face was blank as she moved onto a safer topic of conversation. And that was always the way with her; she was guarded and disciplined, not only with my behaviour, but also with herself and in what she was prepared to share with me. She kept so much of herself back that even now, I think I didn't really know her that well. On the outside she was predictable, rigid day to day, not allowing me to choose what I wanted for dinner, or what I would like to wear. Nor was I permitted more than one sweet per day. There was no spontaneity, no fun. And it seemed she was very strict with herself too; especially when it came to divulging her secrets.

Much later, as an adult, I would read in social services records that Dad had actually paid for me to go into the care of the local authority. And on one occasion, I was taken into care on my second birthday. I have no memory at all of that year, but it saddens me now, to think of myself, aged two, shunted from one foster home to another, whilst my father sat at home alone, too grand or too lazy or simply too male to look after me himself.

"It's woman's work," he liked to say, and the women around him were dutifully silent in reply.

Yet there was another aspect to my mother too and occasionally, just occasionally, she let her mask slip. Sometimes my father worked away, a blissful situation in itself, and at those times, we'd have music on in the house. Mum would dance around the living room, with me twirling and shimmying after her. She loved all the 70s bands; Abba, Brotherhood of Man and Boney M.

"Come on, Sarah," she'd shout, above the music, holding out her hands for mine as she spun me around to *Dancing Queen* and *The Rivers Of Babylon*.

I loved to see that side of her, even if it was just a hazy glimpse. I yearned for that connection. She and I looked very alike; she was petite and slim, with long brown hair, just like me. We sounded uncannily similar too; even Nan occasionally mixed up our voices on the telephone. More than anything, I wanted to be like my mum in character, but how could that be, if I didn't even know who she was? Those joyful moments, singing and dancing, were tragically ephemeral, lasting for two, maybe three songs, then evaporating as abruptly as they'd arrived. No sooner was I allowed a window into my mother's soul, than she slammed a door shut in my face.

"Bedroom," she'd snap, lifting the needle on the record part-way through. "Make sure it's tidy. Your father will be home soon."

The standard routine, when I had done something wrong, even a minor transgression like forgetting to make my bed, was for my mother to put me in the corner until my father came home. He might be home in minutes, or it could easily be hours. Regardless, I was made to stand in the corner and wait. When dad eventually arrived, I had to hold out my hands whilst he hit me with the buckle end of his belt. The punishment was painful, but the anticipation was far worse.

The Letter

Mum never punished me, but neither did she try to save me.

Looking back, I can appreciate she was herself being controlled and abused; she was probably far too frightened of my father to stand up to him. But I was just a small child, and at no time did she ever attempt to help me. She never once let me off a punishment, never made allowances, never softened in any way towards me. She put me in the corner, without enjoyment but also without regret, and I cannot forgive her for taking Dad's side over mine, time after time after time. I think she put me in the corner to save herself, knowing she would get the hiding from Dad, if I didn't. I was a type of shield; my suffering was necessary in order for her to be spared.

****

One weekend, I cannot remember the month or even the year with any certainty, I was staying over at Nan's house, and my parents were also there. We were all sleeping in the same room, where there was a double bed, a single, and a mattress on the floor. Nan had embossed wallpaper, a pattern of raised dots, which I found fascinating. I was just drifting off to sleep, my parents had yet to come to bed, when the door opened, and Dad came in. He touched my arm lightly and told me:

"Go to the bathroom, now."

Not daring to question his command in the darkness, I crept out of the bedroom and into the bathroom opposite. I waited a few minutes, shivering slightly, until Dad appeared. He closed the door and turned the old-fashioned black key in the lock. I had an uneasy feeling in the pit of my stomach, yet with no real sense of why.

"Hold your nightie up," Dad ordered, pushing me roughly against the sink.

He reached round me to run the tap a little and lather his finger with Nan's bar of green soap. It was then that I remembered the Nivea cream, the horror in the caravan, the damp patch on the bed, and I was gripped by an icy dread.

Something in me was outraged that he would help himself to Nan's soap, to Mum's Nivea, to my body. He didn't bother asking. He just took what he fancied. In my confusion and panic, and probably a desperate attempt at denial, I felt more affronted on Nan's behalf than on my own. He had no right to take her soap. None at all. I focussed on the soap as a distraction, the green bubbles, the stinging scent of disinfectant, the perverse association with purity and cleanliness. I told myself it would all be over soon.

Dad leaned over me, and I could smell the cigars on his breath, I heard him groan softly in anticipation. I wanted to scream out, yell for Nan, for my mother, for anyone, to come and help. But the words jammed in my windpipe like pebbles. Dad was wearing jeans and his brown leather belt. He unclasped the belt, and I recognised the clink as it fell, with his jeans, around his knees. Just the same as last time, he put his finger inside me and masturbated. His eyes, always dark, now glittered like two black coals: bottomless, fathomless, pits. There was no end to them and no end to this. I shut my own eyes, desperate to blank him out, waiting for him to be done. But then he said:

"Get onto the toilet."

Abruptly, he lifted me up and sat me on the closed toilet seat. In the next moment my head snapped back against the pipes and the pain shot right up to the back of my throat. It was agony. Dad thrusted back and forth, banging my head against the pipes, ripping my insides apart. Each time I was forced backwards, I saw splotches of memories, no more than broken, unconnected splinters: The meaty hand. The scratchy beard. The blood. A kaleidoscope of pain and betrayal. When it was over, I heard him buckling his belt, and he said matter-of-factly:

"If you tell anyone what I've done, I will shoot the lot of you."

My mouth fell open in horror.

"Why?" I asked. "Why? What have you done?"

Tragically, I did not even know it was wrong. But, just as before, I knew his threat was real. After he had gone, I crept back into the bedroom and cried as quietly as I could, so as not to wake anyone up. Turning on my side, with my stomach throbbing and cramping, I reached out to pop the little bubbles in the wallpaper. One by one, they deflated underneath my fingertip, and each time, I was swamped with sadness and regret. In the corner of the wall was a slight gap where the wallpaper didn't quite meet, and that, too, filled me with despair. Life was imperfect. Life was wrong. Nan's house had always been my sanctuary, my safe place.

My escape from my father. Until now. The next morning, Nan put her hands on her hips and said:

"I wonder who's been popping my wallpaper?"

She winked at me, her eyes dancing with mischief. But I could not muster a smile, even for her. I felt absolutely wretched. On the journey home, I didn't join in the car games. I didn't try to spot the Severn bridge or the pink castle. I could not speak, could not think, could not smile. For weeks afterwards, my only focus was the little bubbles in the wallpaper; flattened, spoiled and lifeless.

Chapter Four

SOON AFTER I turned seven, we moved into the bungalow. Our new home had four bedrooms, a utility area, two
toilets, and Dad had an office. Dad got into ham radio and
became a big fan, spending evenings in his office chatting
to strangers over the radio waves, often arranging to visit
them on the other side of the country. Mum helped clean
the church in her spare time and every now and again we'd
attend Sunday service as a family. Outside the bungalow, we
had lots of land and a large garage.

As the weeks passed, we adopted various animals; one a
white rabbit called Bugsy, who had free run of the garden.
He was always very placid until he spotted the neighbour's
son and would latch comically on to the poor boy's ankle
each time he dared to come through the gate. It was like
watching a cartoon, seeing Bugsy chase him round the
garden. Our temperamental rabbit became something of
a local celebrity due to his split personality and the whole
village had a soft spot for him. We still had our dog, Puff, and
when she had puppies, we gave one to Nan, who named it

Fluff. I'd sneak strays in too; an abandoned baby hare once, who was nurtured under the bed. I smuggled in slugs, slow worms and ladybirds. The old 'swimming pool' from our last home had gone, but there was a posh house in the village where Dad did a lot of renovation work and Mum got a job cleaning, and they had a real outdoor swimming pool.

Even though we were in a different area, Dad had found new customers and seemed to earn well, and we were never really short of money. He had a van for work, but also drove a distinctive burgundy Jaguar, so everyone could spot him from quite a distance. He was instantly recognisable as the friendly local builder and maybe this was an image he culti-vated, to avoid suspicion, or perhaps he simply enjoyed his status. He certainly expected it too.

Whilst our parents were at work at the big house, we were allowed to swim in the outdoor pool. It was a real upgrade on our old well and we couldn't believe our luck. There were steps down into the shallow end, and we had to roll back a plastic cover before we could climb in. We spent the sunny days of our summer holidays jumping in the water, screaming with laughter. Neither of us could swim very well and I wore armbands and a ring. Stephen blew them up for me before each session and made sure I didn't venture too near to the deep end.

The swimming pool was the nearest I ever got to a real holiday, save for the visits to Nan's house. In later years, at high school, Stephen was allowed to go on a school trip to France, but when my turn came around, Dad refused to let me go. Perhaps he worried that, away from home, I might confide in someone about what he'd done to me. Or maybe he just thrived on the control. Still, those afternoons at the swimming pool, seeing who could make the biggest splash, who could hold their breath for longest, were such fun. As usual, Stephen was in charge, and I trusted him completely and implicitly.

"Come on now, Sarah," he'd say, holding my towel ready. "Time to get out and get dressed. It's going to rain."

I enjoyed having a big brother to look out for me. Stephen and I had a close bond. Like many children of that era, we were left to our own devices while our parents worked long hours. We played in the woods near our home, often building elaborate dens. Stephen was strong enough to snap the sticks and tall enough to secure a proper roof. I looked up to him, as every little girl looks up to her big brother. We played games of hide and seek which often stretched out the whole day, until the sun was low in the sky. As the light faded, Stephen would round me up, making sure I got home safely. He was unemotional and straightforward, but at the same time protective and caring. I knew he'd never leave me behind in the woods, no matter what. He didn't ever take my hand, but when I slipped my hand in his, on the walk back, he didn't object.

"I like having you as my big brother," I told him, and was pleased when I spotted him trying to suppress a smile.

The Christmas before our move, I'd got a new bike, and one afternoon, I took it out and cycled quickly over a nearby bridge, skidding off and scraping the basket along the ground. It wasn't badly damaged, but I felt so terrible about it. Mum took one look at me and snapped:

"Get in the corner and wait for your father."

Again, the standard response. She was simply the look-out for our father, not prepared, or not able, to take a decision herself. I was a small insect, caught in a net, waiting for the spider to come back. For hours, I cowered in the corner, my heart jumping in fright when I eventually heard his diesel van chugging to a stop outside. Dad marched through the house, his work boots leaving clods of mud on the carpet which I would later be made to sweep up.

"Hold out your hands," he ordered. "Fingers spread."

Those moments, before the belt made contact, felt like years. The wait was awful. He used the buckle end too, just for good measure. I would never have dreamed of protesting; I was too afraid of my father and, to a lesser extent, my mother, to ever kick back against their discipline. But sometimes, after I'd had the belt, I'd try to catch my mother's eyes, to gauge how she felt about my red, swollen hands, my bleeding fingers, my ripped fingernails. But her eyes were down, her face blank, her feelings boxed up and hidden away. She was so inaccessible, physically and emotionally. She might as well have drawn a curtain around herself and left me out in the cold.

* * * *

School was a 15-minute walk along the coastline to a small and friendly rural primary. And though I wasn't especially keen on written work, I loved art and sport. I was particularly good at cross country running and 1500m track races and was chosen to represent school at the annual inter-schools' sports days. Though I was small and slight, I was nimble, and had a determination and grit which went way beyond my years; developed in part no doubt by my will to survive the turmoil of my home life. I loved long jump, netball, and rounders too. Sport was cathartic for me, a way out and an escape from my own thoughts.

I had a talent for drawing too, and I knew, even at that age, this was what I wanted to do when I grew up. I had a couple of friends in class, but in essence, I was very much a solitary child. It wasn't so much that the other kids left me out, but rather that I distanced myself. And not because I wanted it that way; I didn't prefer my own thoughts, I wasn't even sure I had any thoughts. Maybe, subconsciously, I was emulating my mother, pulling back from any kind of closeness. Or perhaps, more consciously, I kept myself away from other children knowing my life was cataclysmically different to theirs, and knowing my childhood, even during my primary years, was already over.

Because the school was small, there were two classes in each room and so Stephen and I shared the same classroom at certain points. Like me, he was sporty, and was an excellent runner. Sometimes, on the way home, we'd have races, or we'd try to outrun each other in the woods. Two years my senior, Stephen was bigger and stronger and easily beat me every time.

"Just give it up," he laughed. "You'll never win."

But I kept on trying, week after week, month after month. There was something within me that would not give up, no matter what. Stephen was good at cricket too, and he also enjoyed maths and chess. He represented the school at chess and occasionally, Dad would challenge him to a match at home. When I saw the chess set out on the table, I always made myself scarce. Stephen was a better player than our father, but was still too young to understand it was just best to let Dad win. When Stephen proudly announced 'Checkmate' Dad would fly into a rage, upending the board and scattering the pieces.

"I'll be the one to decide the winner!" he yelled, his dark eyes black with fury.

The following December, just before the Christmas break, I was chosen by my teacher to read a Bible verse in church. I was so small for my age that I could barely reach the lectern, and it had to be lowered for me. Even then, I couldn't see out over the top and it caused a ripple of amusement amongst the watching parents.

The verse told the story of King Herod, who had ordered the deaths of many innocent male babies, in his eagerness to ensure that Jesus was killed. It was a gory and gruesome text that sent a shiver through me. It wasn't that I couldn't envisage such cruelty, but more that I knew it existed, right under my own roof. Anything was possible. And so, in the end, I was glad I was not tall enough to look out at the congregation and see my father's black and soulless eyes staring back at me. After the church service, the grown-ups chatted over mince pies and mulled wine, and the children played tag in the darkness of the churchyard. Again, to the outside world, our lifestyle no doubt appeared rather idyllic. We must have seemed like a simple, uncomplicated family, living an uneventful life in a pleasant English village. The irony is so bitter that even now, it chokes me.

After the school term finished, we packed the car and travelled to Aberaeron. I had never spent a Christmas with Nan and Grandad and couldn't wait. In my enthusiasm, I was first to spot the landmarks too.

"There's the bridge!" I called, peering out of the window. "And there's the castle! We're nearly there!"

I could hardly sit still; I was so excited. Even if I didn't get a single present, this would still be the best Christmas ever. Nan had a Christmas tree in her front window, the lights twinkling in welcome as I ran up her path.

"Sarah!" she beamed, opening the door, and pulling me in for a hug. That familiar mix of talcum powder and Welsh cakes filled my nostrils, and I breathed it in. I was home, at last!

"I've been waiting for you," Nan told me. "We've such a lot to do, and it's Christmas Eve tomorrow."

I had, very deliberately, emptied my head of all recollection of the rape in Nan's bathroom. Perhaps it was a survival instinct. It was something I could not make sense of, nor could I change it. And so, I gave it one massive shove, out of my head and out of my world. My mind became a fortress, like the pink castle on our journey here, and bad thoughts were forbidden from entering. It was only when I went to bed that night, and saw the little bubbles in the wallpaper, flattened and popped, that prickles of fear stalked across my skin like marching ants.

Determined not to let the memories back in, I imagined the castle with its drawbridge and moat, and I turned away from the wall and closed my eyes. The next morning, Nan was up early, and we began the Christmas bake. Patiently, she taught me how to make pastry, showing me how to rub the mixture through my fingers until it crumbled easily. Later, the mince pies emerged from the oven, piping hot and beautifully browned, with the mince bubbling through the edges.

"Best pastry I ever tasted," said Grandad, with his mouth full. "I'll have to have another one."

On Christmas morning, I awoke to find a stocking at the end of my bed filled with sweets, raisins, small toys, tangerines and, best of all, love.

"Happy Christmas," Nan smiled, and as I repeated it back to her, I realised that, yes, I was happy. For once in my childhood, I was filled with joy.

Leaving Nan's before New Year was a wrench – worse even than usual because Christmas had been so wonderful. She dabbed my tears with her apron and said:

"You'll be back again soon, love, I'm counting the days."

I was back to visit again, during the following summer holidays. The annual carnival was held in August, and me and my aunts and cousins all dressed as characters from the TV show *Dallas*. My aunt dressed me up as Lucy Ewing, because she was the smallest.

There was a brass band at the carnival, and there were running races for all ages. The carnival queen was dressed in a beautiful gown with a crown on her head, and as I swooned over her jewels, I made a wish that one day, it might be me.

The Letter

Nan gave me money to spend on the stalls, and I bought chips and candyfloss, and had so many turns on the helter-skelter I thought I might be sick.

"Come on," laughed my aunt. "You look green around the chops. Time we all went home."

And for me, that meant Nan's house. My heart and soul were there. And being with Nan and my loving extended family, was like having comforting arms wrapped around me.

Chapter Five

AT THE new house, Dad kept his guns either in his new garage or in his office. They weren't locked away; they didn't even have a designated cupboard. Quite often, he left them lying casually across his desk, as though they were just itching to be used.

"I will shoot the lot of you…"

One was a long rifle, the other was much shorter, a shotgun maybe. As a young girl, I was no expert on guns, but I was certainly old enough to be frightened by them. Dad also had a long sword with a silver handle. Occasionally, he liked to hunt game and foxes, but mainly, he used his weapons to keep me in line. To keep me scared. Every time I saw his gun, I'd remember those chilling threats and I would force the memory of the abuse further down into the bowels of my mind, determined it would never swim back to the periphery. All childhood events: moving house, starting a new school, playing in the woods, were dominated by my fear of my father. He sat, supreme, at the very top of the pyramid, waving a sword in one hand, and a gun in the other. He had total control over everything in our home, and over me most of all.

It wasn't long after we moved into the bungalow that he pounced again. I was watching cartoons on telly one evening, still in my school clothes, when he appeared at the living room door.

"Sarah," he said evenly, with an incline of his head.

That small movement struck terror into my core. I sensed, just from his tone of voice, from the way he held his head, what he had in mind for me. I could feel the danger, smell the foreboding, like rotting meat. Wildly, I looked around me, desperate for an excuse, praying for an escape. But there was no way out. Like a condemned animal, I went obediently to my bedroom. With every muscle clenched, every cell of my body screaming in protest, I lay on the bed, closed my eyes, and willed it to be over.

"You open your mouth, and you'll go back into care," Dad barked, as he buckled up his belt.

I lay on my bed, numb and confused, until the next morning, when it was time to go to school. It did not occur to me to refuse to go, or to tell anyone what was happening to me at home. In my mind, I had a clear picture of those guns. I believed absolutely that my father would carry out his threats. Speaking out was not an option. The following evening, a neighbour came round to look at the latest work Dad was doing on the house, and he whistled in appreciation.

"What a wonderful achievement, building your own home," he said admiringly. "Well done, Bill."

Silently, I listened, marvelling grimly at the chasm between the person my father pretended to be, and the monster he truly was. There was no overlap, no common ground at all between the animal who raped me in my bedroom, and the friendly builder who charmed his customers. I wonder now whether this was all part of his plan. Did he purposely construct another personality to fool people, and to cover his tracks? Or was he actually two people, two characters? Like Bugsy, the rabbit, who loved everyone, but disliked the neighbour's son – did my own father hate me in the same way my rabbit targeted that unfortunate boy? I wished desperately to be able to tap into the other Dad, the life and soul of every party, the builder who couldn't do enough for his community. What was wrong with me that I brought out the very worst in him? Was it something I did, was it a fault in me?

On occasional Saturday afternoons, my parents would go for a drink at the local pub and, if we were good, we went along too. Dad was not a big drinker, except for a few whiskeys at Christmas, but for him, the pub was more about socialising than drinking. I sat quietly at a table with my lemonade and crinkle-cut crisps and watched, in open-mouthed dismay, as Dad worked his way around the room, laughing, back-slapping, joking. Yes, he could look at a damp bathroom next Thursday. Of course, he would price up a kitchen extension, no problem. How could this be the same man? A small part of me wanted to jump up on the bar, smash all the glasses and yell at the top of my voice:

"My dad is a monster! Don't buy him a drink! He does horrible things to me!"

The Letter

But a bigger part of me just wanted him to be like this at home. Despite the horrors I'd already endured, I was always willing to give him another chance. He was my father, and I loved him. All I wanted was for him to love me back.

* * * *

One Sunday evening, after tea, I was having my weekly bath. Facing away from the door, I jumped a little when it opened, and Dad walked in. He didn't speak at all, but just looked at me, and the silence was unnerving.

"What do you want?" I asked eventually, in an effort to deflate the tension.

I assumed he was here to use the toilet. We had a second toilet, near the garage, but it was hardly ever used. Dad was wearing his trademark blue jeans with his leather belt and, as he started to unbuckle, I felt the first sickly prickles of unease. Then, he lifted his chin a little, and despite the warmth of the water, my blood froze.

"I want you to stand up," he said, and his trousers fell to the floor.

I had to do it. His tone of voice made it clear. I had no choice. He was not wearing underwear and he was holding his penis in his hand.

"I want you to wash yourself," Dad said, nodding towards the white flannel, floating in the water.

Trembling, I bent forwards and fished the soap and flannel from the suds.

"All over your chest," he instructed. "Yes, that's right."

I felt excruciatingly awkward. I hated it. But I did as he said.

"Now wash down below," he told me, and I obediently reached down to my knees.

"Not there," he snapped, "further up. Further up."

His eyes grew dark, and panic flashed through me. I didn't know what I'd done to anger him. I was following the instructions as carefully as I could. Rubbing the flannel between my legs, tears streaming down my cheeks, I wished helplessly that it could be over. And then, the door handle rattled a little. The little button lock never worked properly, and suddenly, my mother was walking into the bathroom and Dad was hastily pulling up his trousers and reaching to flush the chain on the toilet. I splashed back down into the water, partly to cover myself but also because I thought that was what Dad expected of me; a level of collusion in something I did not want or understand.

"What are you doing here?" Mum asked Dad.

If there was an accusation in her voice, I did not hear it.

"I was just using the toilet," he replied angrily, already confrontational.

Again, I flinched. I thought it was my fault. Facing away, I scurried up towards the taps, my knees under my chin. Hopefully they would leave me out of it.

"Time to get dried now. Get ready for bed," my mother said.

She looked straight at me, but her eyes seemed to drill right through me to the bathroom tiles behind my head.

"Come on," she prompted, passing me a towel.

The Letter

Wrapping myself in the rough, washed-out cotton, I went to lie on my bed. This was the closest to comfort, or affection, I could hope for.

Not long afterwards, I was playing at the big house, one Saturday afternoon, whilst Dad got on with his building work, and Mum cleaned inside. It was too chilly to swim in the pool, but the house backed onto beautiful woods, and I spent most of the time embroiled in long games of hide and seek. I was at the edge of the yard, on my own, when I heard Dad calling my name.

"Over here," he shouted.

I found him in an outbuilding where there was a ladder going up to a type of open loft, presumably built for storage.

"Go on, up the ladder," he said, nodding impatiently.

I stared doubtfully at the ladder. I was eight years old by now but still small and slight, and the ladder looked huge. The top was, ominously, shrouded in gloom and I shuddered a little.

"What for?" I asked.

But I realised my mistake as soon as I had spoken, and Dad's eyes blazed in the half-light of the shed.

"I said I want you to climb the ladder. So do as you are told," he growled.

Shaking, I climbed the first couple of steps, but they were too wide apart for me. Dad followed behind, shoving me from one rung to the next, his hand on my bottom. At the top, it was dark and dusty, and the structure was only just tall enough for Dad to stand up. He cleared a space, with his foot and I waited uncomfortably, unsure what my task was, until I saw him reach for his belt. Fear switched on like a bright light in my eyes, obscuring all else.

"Take your trousers off," Dad instructed.

"Why?" I pleaded, playing for time. "Why do you want me to take my trousers off?"

An oily dread slid, snake-like, right through me. I was painfully aware I was at someone else's house, partially exposed. Surely, he would not make me do it here.

"Do as you're told," Dad snapped, his eyes black now. "And don't answer me back. Just do it or you know what will happen to you."

I was standing, shivering, in my white knickers and I asked: "Shall I take these off as well?"

As the words left my lips, I cursed myself. Why had I said that? I did not want to take off my underwear, yet still I wanted to please him, I wanted to be helpful.

"Yes," he replied. "All the way, and then lie down."

The floor was very dusty and, as I closed my eyes, I was struck by the overpowering smell of wood. I lay flat, rigid, my small fists balled, my legs pushed tightly together; the only protest I dared to make. There was a rustling noise, a clink and a muffled thud as his belt hit the boards. One hand went over my mouth and, with his leg, he pushed my knees apart. My muscles burned with the effort of trying to resist him, but it was futile. I felt a finger pushed inside me and then something much bigger. A large object was digging in my back, and I thought I was lying on something sharp. Only now, I know the pain was internal, and coming from my father. The second thrust sent a shockwave right through my body and up my throat. I felt myself retching, underneath his hand. And then, filtering through my nightmare, a woman's voice said:

"Is anyone there?"

My heart was clattering against my chest wall, my breath coming in snatches. Dad leaned round to my ear, his beard scratching my cheek, and whispered: "Ssh."

I couldn't have screamed anyway, his hand was over my mouth. Besides, I would never have dared. With my eyes still closed, I listened for the sound of someone climbing the ladder, but as the seconds ticked by, everything went quiet again. She had gone away. I felt at once relieved and disappointed. I longed for someone to make this stop and for my father to be discovered. And yet I did not want to make him angry. I had to keep his secret. When he was confident the coast was clear, he lifted off me, and the weight eased, physically at least. I heard him pulling up his jeans and fastening his belt.

"Get up and get dressed," he said, in a quiet voice. "I don't want you to say a word about this to anyone. You know what will happen if you do."

Dad went down the ladder before me, leaving me in the dusty loft on my own for a moment. My legs knocked together as I shuffled over to the ladder, and I found it hard to find the top rung with my foot. I felt Dad's hand beneath me, taking my ankle and guiding me into the right place.

"Come on, next step," he said, as I climbed slowly down. "Next one, next one."

When I got low enough, he grabbed me and swung me

around, plonking me onto the floor. I flinched each time his hand made contact with my skin, and yet, I craved the proximity. I could not make sense of the two opposing streams of thought, constantly at odds in my head. I brushed myself down, there were wood shavings on my clothes, and Dad did the same. It was, I imagine, a rather touching scene, a father guiding his little girl, helping her down a steep ladder. Yet it was so appallingly contrary to what had just happened. And whilst I did not want my father anywhere near me again, I longed for the attention. I yearned for the approval.

"You'd better go and play," he said.

He walked off and I stood in the yard, rooted to the spot, unable to move, unable to cry, unable to utter a single word. When the light faded, I walked home on my own. Only when I got into bed, that night, did I allow the tears to fall. Nobody ever asked me what was wrong but if they had, I could only have replied that I was unhappy. I did not know why.

Chapter Six

SINCE MY mother worked most evenings, Dad was usually the only adult at home at bedtime, and so there was little to stop him doing exactly as he pleased.

One episode of abuse followed another, and the attacks took on a depressing regularity. They might be as often as two or three times a week and, except for the attacks in the bathroom and at the big house, they were usually in my bedroom or occasionally in his.

Dad insisted that we all changed bedrooms regularly. I don't know whether this disruption was planned with a specific focus, perhaps it facilitated the abuse in some way, or maybe he just wanted to unsettle and upset me. More likely, he simply wanted to remind me who was boss. He insisted, always, that I had to have my bed near to the door, so I could easily slip out when instructed. He always followed the same routine, and the clink of his brown leather belt buckle came to symbolise both the start and the finish of every ordeal. I grew to abhor and welcome that metallic sound, depending on when it occurred. After it was all over, and his belt was buckled again, Dad issued his standard threat.

"You tell anyone, and I'll shoot you. I'll shoot the whole family."

But repetition did not dilute the terror, nor did it dull the authenticity. I believed every word he said, and I carried the responsibility for my family's safety around with me, every moment of the day. I was crushed by it. I might as well have carried a wooden cross on my back, the nails pushed into my hands and feet. As an adult, I have asked myself a million times why my mother did not notice there was something wrong with me during those years of abuse. Many times, I have tried to see it from her viewpoint. She worked evenings, and so she was out of the house much of the time. She suffered from ill-health, she was often in hospital, and even when she was home, she was busy with childcare and housework. More than anything, she was totally preoccupied with her own problems, her health, her marriage, her own despair. I can only presume my own welfare came way down the list, and she never quite got around to worrying about me.

I do not remember ever, in this period, her intervening in anything my father did, or even commenting on the strained atmosphere within our home. Certainly, she never asked me what the matter was. She never once asked me a direct question. My mother did not abuse me, but neither did she look deeper when my father abused me. Self-preservation is both instinctive and powerful so perhaps it even caused her to look away. I will never know for sure.

The Letter

Somehow, alongside this horror, like a smooth path running next to a churning sewer, my life continued. I went to school, did my chores, played with my friends. I learned my times tables and I did my weekly spelling test. I won a medal running cross country for school. In parallel, life ticked along and I never told a soul. I dared not, and besides, what would I say? I didn't even know what the abuse was, or whether it was actually wrong. I accepted it, without question, just as I accepted everything my father did. Perhaps this happened in every household, I decided. It's just what dads do, I told myself. All a part of growing up. The sexual abuse was only an extension of the physical abuse, it was not pleasant, but it was not unusual. Like the thrashings with the belt, it was an aspect of my childhood I just had to endure. I think I knew, then, I was lying to myself, but what option did I have?

Slowly, through the fog of isolation and pain, I forged a way to cope, and a little like Dad's split personality, my own two characters began to emerge. After each attack, I would sit on the end of my bed and shrug, physically bringing my shoulders right up to my ears and filling my lungs with air. It was a huge movement, outside and in, shaking off my old self and leaving a new, blank canvas, wiped clean, in my place. That shrug was so significant, it was like shedding a skin. And as it fell away, so did the memory of the attack. And so, the little girl who went to school each morning was not the little girl who was being abused by her father. School was not an escape, in the most literal sense, because there was nothing to escape from. I had left that child far behind.

At times, the abuse became unbearably painful, and I'd hear my own voice, above me, demanding I defend myself.

"Wake up and fight!" yelled another little girl. "Do something!"

But I was pinned to the bed, paralysed by an agonising fear, and I could not fight back. I couldn't even move. She could yell and scream all she wanted, but I was not as brave as her. Other times, I trained myself to leave my body and float off, somewhere else entirely. I might conjure up the smell of Welsh cakes and imagine I was baking, with Nan, in her cosy kitchen in Aberaeron. Or I'd close my eyes and convince myself I was back at the old house, paddling in the well, the water warmed by the sun.

"Here, Sarah, I'll race you down to the water…"

But my preferred form of escape from Dad's abuse was to plonk myself right in the middle of a *Tom and Jerry* cartoon scene.

With practice, I found I could close my eyes and see a different picture entirely. I followed the cartoon on an imaginary film reel, projected onto my retinas, just as though I was there myself. Transfixed, I watched them chase each around bowling alleys and dining rooms and hotel kitchens, and as they whizzed past me, I felt the rush of moving air. I felt the thrill of the chase. I cheered for Jerry and his efforts to evade capture, but I also felt some sympathy for poor Tom. My favourite episodes were, without doubt, when they joined forces and worked together, because I loved them both dearly. There were several scenes where Tom took a bat and clattered the skirting board, waiting for Jerry to pop out, and it was at this point always that reality and cartoon merged. I'd tell myself that Tom was bashing my Dad, that Tom was here to rescue me, and it was all over. *Sarah is saved by Tom*. It could even have been the name of a classic episode.

I'd wake up, with a half-smile, so immersed in the programme, I had convinced myself the abuse was not happening. Not to me, at least. These attacks were just a horror film from the telly, I'd tell myself. None of it was real. It happened to another girl, and not to me. Yet no matter how hard Tom bashed that wall with his bat, he never caught the mouse. And he never caught my dad.

But there were days when my escapism did not work. Mine was not a fool-proof survival manifesto, it was a desperate and haphazard attempt to cope and, sometimes, it failed me. Often, I couldn't tune in to the cartoon. Neither could I float away on demand. The memory of Nan's kitchen eluded me, the wholesome smells of her cooking were blotted out by the stale stench of sweat and cigars. On those occasions, I would tell myself fiercely that Dad was not my real father, because a true father would not cause me pain like this. No, my real father was out there somewhere, and he loved me dearly. He would come for me one day and take me away from this agony. I only had to be brave and wait.

You'll see, I comforted myself. *He'll knock on the door one day and he'll take you away. He might even take you to Nan's.*

Yet I could never truly embrace this train of thought with much conviction. Because deep down, I loved my father. No matter how much I tried to distance myself, how many lies I told myself, I longed for his affection and his love.

* * * *

My ninth birthday passed, and the attacks continued; a regular and sadistic torture within the four walls of our wonderful home which people admired so much. I wondered even if Dad had constructed this chamber of horrors with me in mind, had he planned his attacks in advance, as he mixed the sand and gravel and laid each brick? Whilst building the house he had incorporated the terror and the suffering, layers of pain and sadness sealed in, alongside the cement. Yet, as I was constantly reminded, we were lucky. Everyone said so.

"Such a lovely garden!"

"Two toilets! So posh!"

"What a great place to raise a family, right on the edge of the countryside."

The compliments were understandable. It was large and airy with so much space. But I felt trapped here, as though I was living in a hermetically sealed box, with the oxygen steadily running out. Even outdoors in the rambling garden, my throat tightened and constricted, and I struggled to breathe. There was no freedom here, no hiding place, no peace of mind.

It was a matter of days before the next attack. Each week bringing more misery and more shame. I did my best to cope, to carry on breathing, to keep the walls from closing in on me. I shrugged the attacks away, I floated up and out of the house, I immersed myself in imaginary worlds. I relied on my old pals Tom and Jerry to get me out of there, and most times, they didn't let me down. When it came to the crunch in cartoon land, they were there for each other, and they were there for me too.

But nobody else was.

I bit my nails, lower and lower, until they were raw and bleeding. When I had no nails left, I found my old Sindy dolls in the toy cupboard and bit off their finger and toenails instead. Of course their digits were so small that I inadvertently bit off whole hands and feet. When I had finished, the mutilated dolls looked like amputees. The jagged holes in the plastic made me feel worse than ever; a physical manifestation of the deep hole into which I was sinking. What had I done? My poor, poor dolls. This was my fault. Again. I knew I was in for trouble, but I also recognised there was no way out of it.

"Why have you done this?" my mother scowled, waving a handless doll in my face. "You naughty girl!"

I had no answer. Or rather, I couldn't put my answer into words. I shrugged my acceptance of my fate, in much the same way as I shrugged off the sexual abuse.

"Get in the corner and wait for your father," she snapped. "Let's see what he says about this."

We both knew exactly what Dad would say, or rather what he would do. True to form, when he arrived home, he thrashed my already bleeding fingers with his belt until tears streamed down my cheeks.

"Let that be a lesson to you," he thundered, as he buckled up again.

Yet much as I tried, I could not stop biting my nails, and

each time mine got too short to gnaw at, I targeted my dolls instead. It was a nervous, anxious habit, and in some small way, it was a release, another survival mechanism. Like my outer body experiences, biting my nails was a way of coping, or trying to cope. Yet I could not escape completely, and my trauma chipped away at me, day after day. I was pulverised, physically and emotionally. Scraped and hollowed out inside, I felt so empty and void, as though there was barely anything left of me. Trudging through my days, carrying my pain around with me, I began to wonder whether I actually existed at all.

Chapter Seven

ONE EVENING, Dad announced, quite out of the blue, that I would be moving bedrooms yet again. In the new room, he pointed out my bed – right next to the door.

"This one's yours," he said. "Perfect for you."

Perfect so that I was easy prey; a little mouse caught in a trap. I thought of Jerry, scampering away from Tom, and reassured myself that he always got away in the end.

Not so for me.

After I had transferred my belongings and my clothes to the new wardrobe and drawers, Dad appeared at my doorway. He didn't even need to speak. I could intuit, from his darkening eyes, from the way he jutted his chin, what lay ahead. He closed the door and then he sexually assaulted me in my new bedroom, on my new bed. It was like a twisted form of baptism. He was making his mark on fresh territory like a feral cat, and in doing so made certain I would never feel safe or relaxed in my own room.

"You open your mouth, I will shoot you and I will shoot your mother," he reminded me, before the door clicked shut.

Afterwards, sore, alone, despairing, I tried to rid myself of the memory, almost as if I was purging my own mind, stripping away all the atrocities that festered there. It was like taking a steam cleaner to the walls of my mind, and it burned just as much. The following morning, like a small robot, the other Sarah went off to school as usual, leaving the first little girl at home in bed. But as the day went on, I found the attack harder and harder to shrug off, every time I blanked it out of my mind, it kept on popping up, like a faulty Jack In The Box.

"I will shoot you and I will shoot your mother."

I worried more about his threats to hurt my mother than I did about myself. Even aged nine, I no longer cared much about my own safety or even my own life. It terrifies me now to acknowledge that even as a child, I had no real motivation to stay alive. My love of life had been stamped out before my childhood had scarcely begun. But the safety of my family was a different matter completely.

I could not have verbalised what was happening to me at home, nor did I understand fully how wrong it really was. Yet even if I had, I could never have risked my mother's life by saying it out loud. Sometimes, I became convinced Dad might shoot Mum regardless, just as a warning to me. Just to make sure I kept quiet. Just because he fancied it. What if he was loading his gun right now, as I sat in class, ready to blast her to pieces as she pegged out the washing? The terror was like a cold hand clutching at my throat.

"Sarah? Are you paying attention to this sum?" my teacher asked. "Can you tell us how many apples are left if two thirds are eaten?"

The Letter

I stared back at her in confusion; perplexed that people around me could focus on such meaningless minutiae when my mother's life was hanging in the balance.

"I don't know, Miss," I mumbled.

At playtime, my classmates chattered and bickered around me while, in something of a daze, I went off to scale the climbing frame on my own. Half-way along, I let myself hang from the monkey bars, swinging back and forth, back and forth, back and forth. I was like a ticking time bomb, waiting to explode. Something had to give.

"I will shoot you and I will shoot your mother."

"Sarah?" called the teacher. "Come on now, time to come back inside. Did you not hear the bell?"

Instead of swinging my way back to the safety of the ladder, I deliberately unfurled my fingers from the bars, allowing myself to fall to the floor. Hovering above, outside my own body, I saw it in slow motion, watching impassively as I landed with a crack and crumpled into a heap on the ground. Within seconds, there was a crowd gathered around me.

"How did it happen? She just fell! Maybe she lost her grip? Is she conscious?"

I didn't speak at all. I couldn't have explained myself anyway. I hadn't planned to let go of the bars, but I had done so on purpose. Maybe I wanted someone to take notice, maybe I was crying out for attention, pleading for help. Perhaps I was trying to cancel out my mental pain with physical pain, an early form of self-harm, maybe even a heartbreakingly ham-fisted attempt to take my own life.

And even now, through the painful prism of experience, I still don't know why I let myself fall.

"Let's get you inside," I heard my teacher say, and she lifted me gently in her arms and carried me into the school office.

After a phone call, she drove me home. I didn't say a word on the short journey. My mother was herself unwell and in hospital that week, and so my aunt was looking after me.

"Let's get you settled into bed," she said, but as I walked into the bedroom, I began vomiting violently.

In my mind, a sketchy link was forming, between the attack in my bedroom and my fall from the bars. It was not one I could articulate, but the foggy patches of memory: the hand on my mouth, the blue bedroom walls, the Nivea tub, the damp patch on the caravan bed, were all connected to this, I knew it. I just didn't know how or why.

My aunt helped me to change my clothes and then called the GP, who sent me to hospital, suspecting a head injury. On the children's ward, tucked up in bed, I felt reassuringly cosy and safe. I had stopped vomiting, and I was feeling much better already. Kermit the Frog paintings smiled at me from the windows, and I smiled back. I liked it here. When a doctor came to examine me, he asked:

"Did anyone hit you, Sarah? Does your dad hit you, at home?"

I shook my head. Another voice, another girl, was pleading with him to ask another question. Perhaps if he got the wording just right, I would crack and tell him the truth, and it would spill out, all over my hospital blankets, this whole, horrible mess. The doctor must have sensed something was

61

not quite right, to ask me the question in the first place. But, satisfied by my denial, he accepted I had fallen from the climbing frame, and he took it no further.

"We'll just have to keep you in hospital for a day or two, because you bumped your head," he explained.

Much later, when I obtained copies of my medical records, they read: *this little girl was admitted to the ward …with a head injury having fallen from a climbing frame. It is unknown whether she was knocked unconscious but had become drowsy and vomited several times…*

I was more than happy to stay on the children's ward for as long as they liked. Looking back, I feel it far more likely my sickness was linked to my trauma, rather than concussion. Like the fall itself, it was my body's clumsy and desperate way of asking for help, a final warning that it could take no more. My aunt came to collect me two days later.

"She's fine to go home now," smiled the nurse. "She seems much more like herself."

I was disappointed as we walked out through the hospital foyer, dreading seeing my father again, and my aunt misinterpreted my low mood as a hangover from the fall. To cheer me up, she bought me a Kermit necklace. It reminded me of the window paintings, of the cheerful nurses, of the safety of those white hospital bedsheets, and I treasured it.

Chapter Eight

IT WAS a slight, almost imperceptible, nod. That was all it took. And with it, my insides liquified.

I had been watching TV, on a perfectly peaceful evening, when Dad appeared at the living room door. His mere presence disturbed the atmosphere like the threat of an oncoming storm.

He tilted his head. He did not even need to speak.

But on this occasion, unlike any other, I felt a sudden and unexpected surge of protest. I did not want this. More than that, I could not go through with it. I just could not put up with it. At my core, I had reached breaking point and I had to draw a line.

I had been abused in my own home, by my own father, since I was a toddler. And I could take no more. I was done with passivity, done with being the victim, done with it all.

There was also a slowly unfurling suspicion that Dad's behaviour was not as normal as I had always believed. Now aged nine, my world was expanding, and my reach was extending beyond my own home. Through school, I had met other families. Watched other fathers interacting with their daughters. And a dissenting, disturbing voice was asking if this did, in fact, happen in all homes and if all dads were like mine. I was beginning to suspect, very strongly, that they were not. Yet it was not defiance or anger which made me ignore him, as he tilted his face, but more a sense of self-preservation. I had reached my limit. I had no choice but to refuse him. Dad lifted his head again, this time jutting his chin slightly, yet there was so much aggression in that small movement. So much malevolence. I could feel his anger crackling across the room, skulking down the side of the sofa, scuttling towards me like a rat.

"Sarah," he said, a warning note in his voice.

"I don't want to," I muttered, my voice barely a whisper. "Please."

Quickly, I looked away, dreading the fall-out, hoping against hope he might just accept it, knowing for certain he would not. Next, he bellowed.

"Sarah. Here. Now."

The acceleration in volume startled me and I sprang bolt upright on the sofa. My stomach was churning but I could not back down now. I had come too far. Yet I knew, also, my brave and foolish plan was built on sand, and he could kick it to bits just as easily as knocking down a child's sandcastle.

The tension stretched taut between us, ready to snap. I tried to focus on the television, but my heart was beating so loudly, I couldn't hear the dialogue. The juxtaposition of the upbeat TV presenter and my father's wickedness jarred something within me. I was, in a way, amazed the programme was still running, as though nothing was happening. I would not have been surprised if my father's control extended to the TV, too, and the presenter suddenly froze in terror.

My father did not speak again, and instead marched over to the brown sofa where I was now huddled up against a cushion, desperate to vanish down through the seams. He walked round behind me and in the next moment I shrieked in shock as he yanked me, by my long hair, right over the back of the sofa and onto the floor. The single movement was breathtakingly painful. My hair was lifting from my scalp. I landed on the carpet with a thud, my back and neck throbbing.

"Get to your room!" Dad bawled. "And don't ever disobey me. Ever!"

He still had a tight hold of my hair and used it to drag me across the room, as though he was pulling a carcass. I felt clumps of hair ripping from my head and the carpet burned my legs and thighs. In the hallway, I struggled to my feet.

"Get your clothes off! Now!" He said.

I began to undress, but found myself back on the floor, unsure whether he had shoved me, or I had collapsed. He kicked me in my side, with the tip of his work boot, and I screamed in agony, my cries coming in short, pitiful batches, while I tried to catch my breath. Ripping off my school clothes, a pinafore and jumper, I was in my underwear by the time I reached my bedroom. Dad grabbed me around the throat and squeezed hard, almost lifting me off my feet.

And despite the pain, despite the panic, I wished fervently that he would only squeeze harder.

"If you ever ignore me again, I'll kill you," he snarled, throwing me onto the bed. Reflexively, his hands went to his belt buckle. Even to my own ears, my cries sounded strange and desolate, like there was a tortured animal, dying inside me.

"I wish you would kill me," I screamed. "Please kill me. Do it!"

My father took a step back and his hand dropped from his belt. Without another word, he turned and left the room, without touching me again.

I don't believe for a minute there was any mercy in his decision. I think he was probably unsettled and alarmed by my outburst and was worried my deteriorating mental state might trigger problems for him. If I was going to kill myself, he certainly didn't want to be implicated. Lying on the bed, it took me a moment to adjust to the silence. But him leaving the room brought me no comfort at all. There was no sense of relief. I was beyond all that. Holding a pillow over my head, I pressed it down hard, intent on suffocating myself. But as my lungs began to burn, I released my grip. I just couldn't do it. I tried again and again, pushing my face into the pillow, willing myself to stop breathing. But each time, as my lungs threatened to explode, I threw it aside, gasping and filled with frustration.

Aged nine, my inability to finish off a suicide attempt only confirmed what I already knew – I was worthless, hopeless, useless. No wonder my father treated me the way he did.

I stashed the attack away with all the others, stacking them up inside me like sharp blades, out of sight, out of mind, but each one capable of causing fatal injury if I moved it even slightly.

A few mornings after my failed suicide attempt, my head still sore, my body covered in bruises, I went outside to feed Bugsy before school, as usual. But as I approached his hutch, I saw immediately something was wrong. He lay on his side, his eyes open and glassy. Gently, I opened the door, and stroked him, but he was already stiff and cold. There was not a mark on him.

"I imagine he was scared by a fox during the night," my mother told me, as we dug a hole to bury him in the back garden. "Literally, he was scared to death. That can happen with animals."

My heart ached for poor Bugsy as I lifted him tenderly into his grave. But her words sent an added chill through me. Was it really possible to die of fright? I thought of the many ways in which my father terrified me, how I was so afraid of him, at times, that I had to remind myself to breathe; in and out, in and out. If it could happen to Bugsy, it could surely happen to me, too. And though the prospect itself was frightening, there was a part of me that saw it as my escape, my way out of the misery.

Chapter Nine

IT WAS maybe a month or two before my 10th birthday, early in 1979, when Dad called me outside into the yard.

"This is Girly," he announced. "My new horse."

"Wow," I said. "She's lovely."

Girly was a grey mare with a gentle temperament, and I liked her, right from the start. I'd always wanted a horse myself, plenty of the farms around us kept horses and I'd often stop on my way home from school, to give them a pat. Dad had been raised with horses, they were a big part of his life, and it was important to him he passed that down to his own children. I think it was probably a narcissistic streak, a desire to create a child in his image, rather than an attempt to give us any pleasure. Stephen was not much interested in horses at all, but I had always been an animal lover. Dad set about building stables, at the side of the house, and while he worked, I'd often put on my wellies and keep Girly company, in her makeshift home in one of the outbuildings.

"Would you like a horse?" Dad asked me one day, as I patted Girly and threw fresh straw under her hooves.

I nodded hesitantly, wondering whether this was a trap of some sort. I knew not to trust my father when he was being nice. And yet, I couldn't help it. I was, after all, a small girl, desperate for paternal approval. A few days later, there was the most handsome Welsh Arab horse standing in the yard, brown with four white socks and a white stripe down his face. He had a black tail and a black mane.

"He's yours," Dad grinned. "What do you think?"

I was over the moon. My first instinct was to run to Dad and throw my arms around him. But I was held back, as though there was a forcefield around him.

"Thank you," I said shyly, my whole face loosening up with my smile.

This was the best gift I'd ever had. And yet, as I hopped from one foot to the other in the yard, conflict uncoiled inside me like a slowly awakening snake. This was the same father who beat me, raped me and made my life unbearable. A horse did not, could not, compensate for that. I knew, too, even then, that there was a clear connection between the abuse and the horse. This beautiful animal was a bribe. A sweetener for me to keep my mouth shut.

"His name is Rosedale Firedancer," Dad told me. "Fire for short. He's a bit of a character so you've got your work cut out. I'm waiting for you to impress me here, Sarah."

I pushed my misgivings to the back of my mind and ran to pat Fire's nose. He was irresistible. But just as dad had predicted, he whinnied and nudged me out of the way.

"Hey," I smiled. "We're going to be pals, just you wait and see."

The Letter

My paternal grandmother, Pam, came over that same weekend to teach me to ride. She was hardline, barking orders and instructions, and scathing of any small progress I made. She was nothing like my Welsh Nan at all. Fire did not help my progress either, he was naughty and temperamental, bucking every time I put the saddle on. He threw me off more times than I could count.

"I'm not giving up," I told him, my face splattered with mud, my arms and legs dotted with bruises.

I was determined to learn to ride, mostly because I loved my horse. But some of it was about pleasing my father, too; I longed for his appreciation and his blessing. Maybe I thought by learning to ride I could somehow bring an end to the abuse; I could make him see I was worth more than that. Inexplicably, after all he had done, I still wanted to make him proud.

"Look," I smiled, as Fire trotted into the yard, me on his back, hanging onto the reins.

Dad nodded curtly, but did not reply. I had more work to do yet. As the weeks passed, Fire calmed down and became more obedient, and my riding skills improved. He was still full of mischief, which I loved. If anyone else went near him, he'd complain and rear up on his hind legs. But for me, he'd lay down so I could tickle his tummy. I taught him to pucker up and give me a kiss too.

"Morning, Fire," I'd say, popping in on my way to school each morning, and he'd reward me with a smacker kiss on my nose.

There was no affection at home, no physical contact other

than the abuse, and so a cuddle with my horse gave me a warmth inside which got me through the day.

Each afternoon after school I was in the stables, mucking out, feeding, scratching Fire's back. I had a bond, a companionship with him that I had never experienced with any human, except my beloved Nan. And when I learned to ride, on my own, the feeling was like nothing else.

As I grew more experienced, I was allowed to take Fire on little jaunts around the local neighbourhood, on my own. Cantering through fields, the wind in my hair, was exhilarating. I felt energised and cleansed and it was in some small way an antidote to the sexual abuse. Dad's attacks left me feeling dirty, listless and trapped. But outdoors, with Fire, I felt such freedom. And having a horse brought me a measure of independence too. I had a schoolfriend in the next village who had her own horse. At weekends I rode Fire across the fields to see her and we went out riding together. There were several families with horses in our village; it was made up mainly of small-holdings, cottages and farms, and, through Fire, I got to know all the girls around my age. Sometimes, I'd be invited into their homes for a glass of cordial or a biscuit. I met their parents and siblings. I soaked up the familial atmosphere, noting the lack of tension, the absence of fear. These families were all so different to my own and it only reinforced my growing suspicion that what took place in my own home was wrong.

I had one friend in particular, named Molly, whose parents were so transparently wholesome and loving, that I became at once reluctant and desperate to visit. I longed to share in that tenderness, to be welcomed into the heart of their family. But a part of me resented that Molly had the very thing I craved, and I was eaten up with an envy I found hard to contain. One Saturday morning I had arranged to meet her, to ride out with the horses, but I was strung up with worry and anxiety about my father's abuse, which showed no signs of stopping or even slowing.

"What's up with you?" she asked, as I trotted into the yard. "You don't look yourself."

Her voice was filled with concern and kindness, and I felt myself cracking and wavering. Could I confide in her? Would she understand? Maybe her parents might even help me. I had a brief, glorious, image of a scenario in which I might escape my father's regime and my mother's indifference.

"Molly," I began, and hesitated.

"Look, hang on a sec," she said. "I just need to nip back inside for my hat. Watch the horse for me. We can talk while we ride, and you can tell me all about it."

I waited in the yard, in-between our two horses, with my heart thrashing about like a wild animal. I was seconds away from sharing my secret. Could I really go through with it? A wall of strength and courage was building, brick by brick, in my chest. *You can do this.* And then, behind me, I heard the familiar chug of my father's diesel van.

"What are you doing here?" he asked, out of the driver's window.

I was dumbfounded to see him. I was half convinced it was some sort of telepathy, that he had sensed I was about to defy him and was here to stop me. Maybe he was even here to shoot me. My mouth ran dry at the thought.

"I'm just seeing Molly," I stuttered. "We're taking the horses out."

Dad nodded.

"You make sure you behave yourself," he said darkly, before turning the truck around and driving away.

"What did you want to tell me?" Molly asked, appearing at my side.

But it was too late. My wall of courage was smashed to pieces, bulldozed by Dad's visit. I could not believe I had been tempted to betray him, it was so foolish, so dangerous, to even consider it.

"You open your mouth and I'll shoot the lot of you."

After I grew up, I realised Dad's visit was perfectly predictable and easily explained. It was a Saturday morning and he was on his way to work, driving right past Molly's house on his usual route out of the village. No doubt he spotted me from the road and thought it would do no harm to check up on me and remind me of his threat. But for years, as a child, I remained convinced there was some supernatural force at work, that Dad not only controlled my actions, but now my thoughts as well. An omnipresent force, an all-seeing devil, I would do well never to cross him, not even subconsciously. Feverishly, I began filtering my thoughts, emptying my head, blanking out all feelings, all opinions, all signs of life within me. Only when I was with Fire did I rally a little. He painted the colour back into my grey and lonely world.

"Don't know what I'd do without you," I sighed, as he lay on his back, his tummy exposed, demanding a tickle.

As time passed, Dad encouraged me to enter local shows and gymkhanas. I learned to groom Fire, plait his mane, walk him round a ring and trot him round a field. Mum plaited my own hair, just like his, and I wore smart jodhpurs and a blue jacket with a black velvet collar.

"You look really nice," Mum smiled, with a rare compliment.

And I felt it, too. I felt capable and worthy, as though I was, at last, useful in some way. I won rosettes at Tytherleigh and Somerton horse shows and at Chilcompton gymkhana. By the end of that first year, I had a drawer full of rosettes and trophies. By now, Puff, our family dog, had passed away and we got a labrador named Goldie. I trained her and won awards at the local shows for dog-handling. But my real love was horses, and I so looked forward to those days out with Fire. We even went to a show one day where we spotted Harvey Smith, the famous showjumper. And I caught sight of the Blue Peter horse from the telly.

"Look Dad!" I beamed, pointing out the rows of horses, freshly groomed and decorated with ribbons and bows.

On these occasions, Dad was in friendly builder mode, fully in character, just as surely as if he was acting on a big stage. He laughed and joked with the other parents, admired the children's horses, whooped and cheered when I won prizes. I savoured those moments and wished they could last forever. Yet in the pit of my stomach, there was a gnawing angst, a sad acceptance, that this would not last.

One day, at a show, Dad's horse, Girly, had misbehaved and failed to win any of her categories. I could feel Dad's temper brewing, like mercury rising up a thermometer. He waited until we were away from the crowd, hidden by the side of the horsebox and then he aimed a hard punch at the horse's neck.

"You useless bloody animal," he snarled, as she whined in pain.

My hands itched to soothe her, but I was too afraid. I would much rather my father had hit me than his horse, and I despised my own lack of courage, that I wasn't brave enough to stand up for the poor animal. There was nothing I could have done. He would likely have hit her twice if I had intervened. But that didn't ease my guilt.

"I'm sorry, Girly," I whispered later, when she was back in the stables.

Dad gave me a riding crop one day, and insisted I use it to lash Fire when he was misbehaving.

"An animal needs to know who is boss," Dad told me. "It will behave better if you whip it every now and again."

He seemed to have pretty much the same approach with his own daughter. But though I was wary of disobeying Dad, I couldn't bring myself to hurt my horse. Luckily, Dad was too disinterested to come out in the field with me, and preferred to stand at the gate, yelling instructions.

"Use your crop! Let him have it!"

I worked out I could bring the crop down heavily on my own riding boot, making it look and sound as though I was hitting Fire. In the distance, Dad was easily fooled.

"That's it," he shouted approvingly. "Give him another one. He's settling down."

Fire and I shared a secret snigger, and it strengthened our bond even more.

My involvement with the horses did not, as I had hoped, help in any way to calm Dad's volatility or his perversions. The sexual abuse continued, just as before. And now that he had horse whips, he used those, along with his belt, to punish me. One day, I was having a ride out with Fire, before a horse show, when he threw me, head over heels, in a field which had recently been spread with manure. I was covered in the stuff. I looked and smelled so bad that even Fire gave me a sideways glance as I walked him back to the stables.

"This is all your fault," I told him with a giggle. "Hopefully Dad won't see the state of me."

But my heart sank when I spotted him waiting in the yard.

"What the hell have you been doing?" he bawled. "We're supposed to be at the show in an hour."

Luckily, I had a spare pair of jodhpurs to change into, and after a bath, I was ready to go. Dad though, made sure there was time to lash my hands with the horse whip, leaving a weal across my fingers.

"Don't do it again!" he shouted, as though I was in the habit of throwing myself into manure.

The horse show passed without any of the usual appeal for me, and the smell hung around me for days afterwards. No matter how much I washed and scrubbed, I couldn't quite get rid of it. It was a reminder of my father's cruelty and more broadly, of the injustice of the whole situation. Like the abuse, I feared the manure might become ingrained into my skin, another layer, another trauma, from which I would never escape.

****

Early one Saturday morning, I was clearing out the horse-box, ready for a show later that day. It was a double size box, so the two horses could stand side by side as they travelled. With my brush in my hand, I was daydreaming about a first prize rosette, when Dad climbed in through the side door. He pulled it shut, with a bang, behind him. It was just me and him, and the ripe, heavy smell of the horse box. Immediately, alarm bells rang. I did not need to raise my head to see his black eyes, his head tilting slightly.

"Doing a grand job here," he said, with a weird smile.

This was all part of his well-practised routine. A hideously repulsive attempt to be nice to me, a smile or even a mirthless laugh, before he got down to business.

Please no, I told myself silently.

Outwardly, I said nothing.

Mercifully, the sexual assault was over quite quickly, and I retched as he relieved himself in a pile of straw, which I would then have to sweep up and compost. It felt like the final ignominy. It was not enough for him to assault me, I had to clean up after him too.

"You tell anyone, I will kill you," he said, as he buckled his belt.

For some reason, probably because it was outdoors, this

attack felt more demeaning and humiliating even than the others. Afterwards, I slumped to my knees, folded over on myself, and wept. There were people passing through the yard and my mother was in the house, just a few metres away. Someone could have driven into the yard at any point, knocked on the horsebox, even rattled the door. And yet my father did not seem to notice. Perhaps his perverted desire got the better of him, and he decided he couldn't wait. But I think rather he was so arrogant and brazen, that he simply did not care. So what if my mother, or anyone else, challenged him? He was untouchable. By the time I had finished sweeping out the old straw, I had somehow shrugged off the attack, rolled back my shoulders, emptied my lungs, and told myself it never happened. It was a movie, it was a different girl, it was a figment of my imagination. It was nothing to do with me.

"Shrug it off," I told myself firmly. "Just shrug it away."

Days later, I was in the stables with Fire, when Dad appeared and banged the wooden door shut. My heart dropped, like a falling boulder, into my boots. *Please no,* I begged silently. *Anywhere but here. No.*

"Pull down your trousers and knickers," he ordered. "Lie down, there."

The stable was my sanctuary, the only place where I was content, the only place where I could be a child. Dad knew that. He raped me there out of sheer spite, out of cruelty, just because he knew he could. I think he thrived on the control, more so even than the sexual gratification. Maybe for him, it was all one and the same.

Throughout, I heard Fire whinnying in frustration and stamping his hooves, his big, concerned eyes looking down at mine. He could sense my distress yet could do nothing to help. Closing my eyes, I concentrated on levitating up, out of my body, to the rafters in the roof. Now, I was looking down on the scene, staring at the backs of Fire and Girly, unsettled and anxious in their stalls, and at myself, lying on top of the straw, my father crushing me with his bulk as I suffered the worst violation imaginable.

That's not me, I reassured myself. *It's another girl. It's definitely not me.*

The location of the rape was worse even than the rape itself. I had spent so many happy hours in the stables and now, they were spoiled, and the memories were polluted. My father wanted to pull apart every aspect of my childhood and ensure I had no good memories left at all. But why? Why was he so intent on ruining me? When the trademark clink of his belt buckle signified the end of my distress, I plummeted back down from the roof, back into my body, and covered my face with my hands.

"You breathe a word, and I will shoot you," he said, and oh, how I wished he would.

The buckling of his belt might well mark the end of one attack, but in a way, it symbolised the start of the next too. There were so many, they all merged into one, unbearable mess. There were more attacks in the stables. It was all about opportunity, as well as gratification. If my father spotted that I was on my own somewhere, he took his chance. I grew to dread going into the stables, knowing I was an easy target, and yet, nothing could have prevented me from doing so. Fire needed food and water and clean straw. Besides, I loved spending my spare time with him; he was my best friend. The stables were my refuge. I knew as well that if not there, then my father would have attacked me elsewhere. There was no escape.

Even in the solitude of the stables, I never breathed a word about the attacks, not to Fire, and not to myself. I was too afraid to say it out loud. And yet, there was an unspoken acceptance between me and my horse, a togetherness, a shared suffering. We harboured a most shocking secret and only he and I and the walls themselves truly knew what kind of monster my father was. As we rode through the fields and woods, I felt osmotic waves of compassion and love permeating through Fire, through the saddle, into me.

I am here for you, Sarah. I know what you're going through.

I loved him for it. I appreciated and valued him, more than he could ever know. Fire was my horse, my best friend, my therapist and my saviour. And so conversely, my father's attempts to destroy me by raping me in the stables had backfired spectacularly. Now, I was fighting fire with Fire. I had my horse on my side.

Chapter Ten

ONE MORNING, soon after my 11th birthday, I was getting dressed ready for school when Dad poked his head around my bedroom door. To my relief, he was dressed in his work boots and heavy coat and his van keys dangled from his hand. He was obviously not here to attack me.

"You're having a day off school," he announced. "Your mother's unwell, some sort of reaction to her new tablets. You need to be here to keep an eye on her. I'm going to work."

I was rather pleased with the news, I was in my final year at primary school and, like most of my classmates, was more than ready for the transition to high school. I quite fancied a day at home, as long as Dad was out. Peeping into Mum's room, I saw immediately she'd had a severe allergic reaction, there was a mottled rash creeping up her neck and onto her swollen face.

"Do you want some breakfast?" I asked. "I could do you some tea and toast? Or a bowl of porridge?"

Mum's eyes were glassy, as if she couldn't really hear me.

The Letter

"Mum?" I prompted. "What about a glass of water?"

"Chips," she muttered, through bloated lips. "Chips."

It seemed to be the only word she could say, and I wasn't sure chips were the best choice for her. I left her for an hour to sleep, whilst I went to clear the breakfast pots and sweep the kitchen lino. I put a wash on and hoovered the hallway, before going back to check on Mum. This time, her eyes were almost closed, and her face was more puffed up than ever.

"Chips," she said again.

"Oh Mum, I think maybe we should get you some help," I frowned.

I ran out the front door and knocked on our nearest neighbour's door.

"Can you come and look at my mum?" I asked, knowing Dad would likely blow his top when he found out I'd brought someone into the house without his permission. But I was so worried about Mum, I had to take that chance. Our neighbour took one look at Mum and decided we should call the doctor. When he arrived, shortly afterwards, he rang for an ambulance.

"Where's your father?" the doctor demanded. "He really should be here."

Mum went off to hospital and I was relieved she was at least in the right place, and also that I had clearly done the right thing. Hopefully, I would avoid punishment. When Dad came home, I had lamb chops and mash waiting for him, and he seemed to take the news about Mum quite well. I dared to relax a little. But at bedtime, as I was brushing my teeth, Dad called my name.

"Sarah?"

Just the tone of his voice set my nerves on edge. When I went to his bedroom and saw his eyes darkening, my heart crashed downwards. *Please, no.*

"You're going to be Mum for the night," he announced, as though I had won some sort of sick prize.

He gestured to her side of the bed where, on the bedside table, was a traitorous pot of Nivea.

"Take your nightie off," Dad said. "Get into bed, Mum's side."

In dismay, I did as he said. Inwardly, I was screaming, railing against this latest atrocity. Outwardly, I was silent. The cloying scent of Nivea pricked the back of my throat, as Dad creamed his finger, before beginning the assault. I closed my eyes, searching through my memory bank for a favourite episode of *Tom and Jerry*, or a treasured recollection of making pastry with Nan, my hands and face floury.

"You're doing a grand job, Sarah, make sure you roll it out evenly now."

Snapping back to reality, when it was over, I heard Dad say: "Go on, back to your own bed, right away. You keep your dirty little secret, or you know what will happen. You know I will kill you."

I scampered back to my cold bed, my thighs stinging, my stomach cramping. Desperately, I tried to tune back into Nan's kitchen, but the picture was frozen and fuzzy. The connection was gone. I stared into the darkness, the nothingness, with Dad's words echoing round my skull.

"…*your* dirty little secret."

Clearly, it was my secret and not his. So it had to be my fault. This was confirmation, if any was needed, that I was the one in the wrong.

"You know I will kill you."

With all my heart, as I lay in the dark, I really wished he would. This was no longer a threat; it was a way out. It would have been a welcome release if my father killed me. I had again reached the point where life frightened me more than death.

****

That September, I was due to start high school, and along with my classmates, I was preparing for the big move. Despite myself, I was quite excited. I was looking forward to a new start, new uniform, new teachers. But during the summer holidays, Mum announced she'd hit a snag.

"The high school is less than three miles away," she said. "So you don't qualify for the school bus. You can't walk; it's dangerous, there are no footpaths on the country roads. Your Dad is busy working, and I don't have the car."

"What does that mean?" I asked. "How am I going to get to school?"

She pursed her lips.

"We've decided you can go to school in Aberaeron, until we get something sorted out."

As her words dawned on me, I was filled at first with enthusiasm.

"I'm going to live with Nan again? Amazing!"

But as reality settled, I realised they were getting rid of me. It seemed to me like Mum was finding ways not to be able to get me to high school. She was looking for problems, and not solutions. I was being shipped out, palmed off on my Nan, once again.

Now, I wonder whether Mum was actually trying to save me, to get me out of the way of my father. Did she know or suspect what was going on? At the time, her matter-of-fact approach felt like a slap in the face. Our bond, already stretched thin like an old elastic band, felt it might snap and ping back into my face. But, as the days passed, I tried to focus on the positives. I couldn't wait to spend time with Nan, and in Aberaeron, I was loved and cared for. Best of all, I was away from my father.

Mum bought me a new uniform, shoes and a satchel, ready for the start of term. We drove down in late August, and Nan's little village looked as inviting as always, bathed in sunlight, with the sea shimmering in the distance.

"I've been so looking forward to you coming to stay," Nan beamed. "Your bed is ready."

I settled back easily into the routine of living with Nan and Grandad, the whist drives, the trips to the park, the ongoing drama of the soap operas.

"I can't believe she's ended up with him," Nan would say in disgust, flicking the TV off. "I'm not watching it again."

But the next night, we'd both be there, glued to the screen, anxiously awaiting the next instalment. We did lots of baking, and I perfected my pastry-making. At home, cooking was a chore. But at Nan's, I enjoyed trying out apple pies and biscuits and Welsh cakes. Again, I puzzled over the differences between the two households, and I didn't understand how Nan managed to make the most boring jobs seem like such fun.

"I'll wash, you dry," she'd say, throwing me a tea towel, and I'd happily oblige. She just had a way of making things seem better, lighter somehow.

Nan had a brown striped cardigan which I borrowed so often she eventually let me have it. It was far too big for me. Even aged 11 I was still slight and slim. The sleeves hung down over my hands and it was too long. But I loved it. The wool smelled of Nan, of Lily of the Valley, of kindness and of love. Putting on the cardigan was like having her arms around me. I wore it on a day out one weekend and Grandad took our photo.

"Here," he said, handing me the print. "One for your album."

I treasure that photo still. Me and Nan, and the brown cardigan. I look at the happiness on my face and remind myself my childhood was not all bad. The high school was not nearly as daunting as it might have been, because I knew some of the children there from my short stint at the primary school, five years earlier. Nan and Grandad had a big family, they were well known locally, and so I was welcomed by association. I settled in and soon began to enjoy school. My only fear was that this life would not last. One day, my parents would be back to claim me.

"I wish I could stay here forever," I told Nan dreamily. "I love it at your house."

"It's the sea air," she replied, with a smile. "It's so good for you. Your cheeks are rosy, and I think you've grown a bit. You were quite peaky when you arrived, you know. I was a bit worried about you."

Much as I wrestled with my inner demons, I could not begin to tell her the truth. There were times when Dad seemed so far away, that his threats were somewhat diluted. I had such faith in Nan, I felt she, if anyone, might be able to save me. But I could never quite pluck up the courage to tell her. I didn't have the words, and I was also too frightened to look for them. Besides, I knew the revelation would break her heart. When Dad visited Nan, he was always in 'charming builder' mode, full of jokes and wisecracks, eager to help out.

"You could charm a rattlesnake," she used to tell him.

To others, it was charisma. To me, it was brainwashing. And he used his engaging other self as a cover for the monster that hid beneath. She would not have been able to cope with the shocking reality of his other self. She knew, however, something of his violence towards Mum. Perhaps Mum had confided in her, or maybe she'd seen it for herself. Occasionally, she'd ask me if they were getting on OK, or if there were any rows at home. I wanted to put her mind at rest.

"Everything is fine, Nan, honestly," I'd smile and say.

If ever I was tempted to say more, I'd think of those two guns lying casually, menacingly, across Dad's desk, and my resolve evaporated.

"Open your mouth and I will shoot you all."

The Letter

From September to December, I didn't see my parents at all. They didn't visit once. But there was usually a weekly phone call from Mum, where I'd bombard her with questions about Fire, and make her promise me she was looking after him. Dad would insist on a brief word at the end:

"Just checking you're behaving yourself?"

Hearing his voice struck fear into me, and I realised, with a rush, how foolish I had been to even consider confiding in Nan. Dad's threats were real, and I could not afford to take any risks. Those short conversations were his way of making sure I kept quiet. He was like a vulture, peck, peck, pecking away at what remained of me. But even aged 11, I felt I had been dead inside for so long now, that there was very little left for him to take.

Chapter Eleven

THE DAY after the school term finished for Christmas, my aunt visited.

"Surprise! I've come to take you home for the holidays," she announced. "Isn't that brilliant?"

My face fell. I had hoped to spend Christmas in Aberaeron, with Nan. But I also missed Fire so much and was anxious to see him. I comforted myself with the idea of being around him on Christmas morning, even smuggling out some treats for him.

"Pack a bag," my aunt said. "Don't forget anything. It's a long way."

I was torn, but I had no choice and so off I went upstairs, with the assurance I'd be allowed back to Nan's in the New Year.

"Happy Christmas!" Nan smiled as we left. "You say hello to everyone for me."

We arrived back in Somerset on the afternoon of Christmas Eve, and I ran into the stables first, my heart bursting with love when I heard Fire snort in excitement. He rewarded me by falling comically to the floor and rolling so I could tickle his tummy.

"I'm back," I beamed. "I've missed you, pal."

I delayed going into the house for as long as I could, and within moments of stepping through the door, I was longing to be back with Nan. The house was busy and noisy and filling up with relatives. We had cousins staying overnight too. My only comfort was that Dad would not be able to get me on my own in all this chaos. In the evening, the adults went out to the pub and while they were gone, Stephen, then aged 13, and another cousin, decided to peek at the presents under the tree.

"Don't," I protested. "We'll all be in trouble. You know how angry Dad can be. You know what he's like."

Stephen was showing off and he waved me away, like the annoying little sister. He started off by tearing just a corner of wrapping paper or lifting an inch of Sellotape. But it became addictive and soon, he and the cousin were gleefully ripping open gifts which could not be easily rewrapped. When our parents arrived home, confronted by discarded wrappings and ruined surprises, Dad was furious. We were lucky that we had visitors staying, and so we were spared the belt and the whip. Even so, he was livid with us.

"Christmas is cancelled!" he thundered. "No presents. That's final."

We trudged off to bed, the Christmas spirit well and truly extinguished. I hadn't even peeped at a single present, but I was well used to being punished for things I had not done, and it barely registered with me.

Now I was back home, a toxic smog of depression hung around me like a virus. I could not muster much enthusiasm, even at Christmas. Again, I felt like I had two incompatible personalities and the girl who was so full of joy and happiness was left behind in Aberaeron. The following morning, Christmas Day, Dad relented to allow us one gift each, again, a concession brought about only by our visiting relatives. He was always keen to maintain his 'charming builder' persona around other adults, though this time, he had clearly been pushed to the limit. My own gift was a flute, a beautiful silver instrument in a black case with velvet padding. I had been asking for a flute for months, I was so eager to learn to play. I'd already inquired about music lessons at my new high school. It was a lovely gift, far more extravagant than I was used to, even at Christmas. And yet, there was a dullness inside me, a flat, defeated feeling, and I just could not drum up the usual festive joy.

"Thank you," I said politely. "It's very nice."

After dinner, all our guests left and went home. Early in the evening, I went to bed. My bedroom had been swapped again, on Dad's orders, and this time I was in a little room at the end of the hallway, on my own. Lying in bed, in the dark, on my back, I dozed and drifted in between consciousness and sleep. In a daze, I was vaguely aware of the bedroom door opening, and softly closing again. I sensed there was someone else in the room and quickly, horribly, I was wide awake.

Suddenly every nerve end in my body was jangling, every pore in my skin was on high alert. I dared not speak, hardly dared even breathe. Maybe, if he thought I was asleep, he would leave. I waited, but he did not say a word. There was no light, and I couldn't see him, couldn't even make out his outline, through the darkness. And yet, I could hear breathing. I knew it was my father's breathing. I would have known it anywhere. There was a low murmur and then, in one fluid movement, he swiped my blankets from the bed and onto the carpet. The cold air rushed up around my legs and, gagging in fear, I swallowed back my nausea.

"Shhh," he ordered, pulling up my nightie.

As he climbed on top of me, I felt all my limbs would snap. He felt heavier than ever. The smell of cigars hit the back of my throat and made me retch again, and his hand landed like a clamp over my face, covering my mouth completely. His beard, a small goatee, was up against my chin and it was scratchy and rough. Still I could see nothing. I felt his fingers, sharp and painful, pushed inside me. As it went on, he got heavier and heavier. I had the impression I was sinking down, through the sheet, through the mattress, through the floor. How I wished I could somehow tunnel away from this. But there was no escape. Instead, I was pinned to the bed, my heart hammering and banging against my ribcage.

Still without a word, without any warning, his fingers withdrew, and then an excruciating pain shot right through me. In shock, I opened my eyes, and there, in the darkness, his black eyes gleamed and glinted. It was like looking into the eyes of a savage beast. When it was over, I heard the faint clink of a belt being buckled, and in his normal voice, he said:

"If you tell anyone what has happened, I will take away your new flute. Then I will take my gun from my office, and I will shoot you all."

With that, the door opened and closed, and he was gone. I lay on the bed, glued to the mattress, too petrified, too appalled, to even cover myself up. My nightie was crumpled up around my waist, and my blankets lay on the carpet for the rest of the night. Tears leaked from my closed eyes, onto the pillow. I was freezing cold and yet it didn't even register with me. I didn't feel anything except an all-consuming, intolerable agony.

I didn't want a flute for Christmas. I just wanted to die. That was my Christmas wish. Death. I had not seen my family for four months, and yet, within hours of me arriving home, it had started again. I could not work out what I had done to deserve such a father. To merit such suffering. I had not seen him. I had not spoken with him. Yet like a ghoul in the night, a passing, venomous fiend, he had stolen what he wanted and left.

In the New Year, I returned to Nan's house, with the flute. I did not dare leave it behind. On the first day of the new term, she called the school and booked music lessons for me.

"I knew you'd be pleased," she smiled. "I'm looking forward to putting in some requests of my own when you can play."

I smiled weakly, despairing yet appreciative, in equal measure. Everything she did, she did out of love for me. For her sake, I went through with the lessons, but I hated every second of them. I could not bear to look at my flute without remembering the rape. The darkness, the anonymity of the attacker, had spooked me to my soul, and to me, the flute was mixed up in the horror of it all. Even in the midst of it, I recognised the tragedy of a beautiful instrument, and an innocent child, becoming synonymous with such grotesque suffering and perversion.

* * * *

I spent the remainder of the school year in Aberaeron, and from January to July 1981, my parents did not visit once. We kept in touch over the phone, or, as I see it now, my father made sure I kept my mouth shut with regular phone calls:

"You make sure you behave yourself there, Sarah. Don't let me down."

I did not miss my parents at all, and as a child, I felt guilty and confused that I didn't think of them much. Was I abnormal, ungrateful, detached in some way? It didn't occur to me that the blame lay with them, that the lack of a bond with their own daughter was a glaring failure all of their own.

I was homesick only for Fire, my faithful friend, and I missed him dreadfully. In my daydreams, there was a world where Fire miraculously came to live in Aberaeron with me, tucked up in Nan's garden shed alongside the plant pots and the lawnmower. I'd have let him share my bedroom if it meant he could live with me. That would have been my version of utopia; Fire and me, living with Nan forever. But then Mum called, with news that a decision had been made for me, as usual, without asking what I thought first.

"You can go to the local school next year," she announced. "Your Dad can drop you off in the mornings. He's managed to fit in the school run with his work after all. So you can come home for good."

I had always feared, deep down, it wouldn't last. I never believed my father would let me escape his clutches so easily. When the school year ended in the summer, I was divided. I was desperate to be with my horse. And though I didn't for one minute relish the prospect of going home, I wanted my parents to want me. I longed to feel loved. But leaving Nan's was a dreadful blow, too. I'd been here so long, I'd made friends, and I'd allowed myself to enjoy and expect this life, this feeling of safety and belonging. I had become complacent, reliant upon what was essentially a simple and normal lifestyle. And now, like a macabre magic trick, the rug was being pulled from underneath me, upending everything I knew and loved.

When Mum came to collect me, there was no light in her eyes. None in mine either. I packed my stuff and said my goodbyes to Nan and Grandad, and my heart was heavy as Nan hugged me for the last time. This would be the last hug I'd get for a long time. As we drove away and the Severn bridge loomed into view, I already felt homesick for Wales.

"You'll settle in at the new school, you'll see," Mum said.

I didn't know how to tell her that it was my home, not the school, that I was worried about. It wasn't the new teachers or even the new kids that concerned me. It was my own parents.

I enrolled at the local school that September, and I caught

up with a few old pals. I settled in, though I felt happier on my own, much of the time. I loved seeing Fire every day again, I had missed him more than I could have thought possible, yet nothing could make up for the chasm created by me leaving Nan.

I had been home only a matter of days when Dad appeared at my bedroom door, his chin tilted and his eyes dark, and my spirits sank. In my heart, I had known this would happen, yet a small piece of me, foolishly, naively, had hoped perhaps he would leave me alone. Instead he simply picked up where he had left off, as though the sexual abuse was as much a part of his daily routine as watching the nightly weather forecast.

Being away at Nan's and enjoying some respite had made it even harder to cope with when it started again. I now realised, with disgust, with barely concealed repulsion, how wrong and rancid this was in every way. I desperately needed an escape, an outlet, but did not know where to turn. Moving schools frequently meant I didn't have an especially close bond with any friends or teachers. There were no staff members at the new high school who even seemed particularly interested in me, there was nobody who I might consider trusting with my secret. And every time I thought of confiding in someone, each time I reached an emotional boiling point, I remembered the way Dad had appeared, like a ghoul, in Molly's yard, and I reminded myself this was not a battle I could win.

"You tell anyone and I'll kill you. And I might kill your mother as well."

Not long into the new term, I was sitting in class one

afternoon when a boy behind me flicked a ball of chewing gum, and it landed in my long hair. Later I went home with a sticky, knotty mess at the back of my head. Dad was outraged. He had always insisted I kept my hair long, I was not allowed to have it cut at all, right through my childhood. My own preferences didn't come into it. Whether this was an aspect of his sexual deviance, or it was more about control, I still don't know. My long hair made me look very much like my mother, though hers was usually loose and mine was in pigtails. I wonder whether the similarity was an image which fuelled Dad's perversions. Did he hate the resemblance, did he love it, or was it all the same thing to him? But this time, with my hair balled up into a gluey lug, even he could see that drastic action was needed. Mum took me straight down to the local hairdresser, who tidied my hair up into a short bob.

"It's a mess," Dad growled, when we got home. "You need to grow it back."

In truth, I cared little about my appearance. In contrast to my friends, many of whom were on the cusp of puberty and falling in love for the first time, I had no interest in boys. No time at all for romance. I didn't wear make-up and I wasn't bothered what kind of clothes I wore. My wardrobe was, as when I was small, made up of disparate items from jumble sales and charity shops. I wore hand-me-downs from relatives. And I wasn't in any way embarrassed – rather, I cultivated it. I didn't want to look pretty or fashionable or appealing. I wanted to be anonymous.

Usually, after school, I changed into my riding jodhpurs

and a frayed old jumper, ready to work in the stables. I was keen not to attract attention, and my father saw to it that I didn't. As much as I could, I tried to ignore the changes in my body, I wore baggy clothes, unflattering underwear, and I rarely looked in the mirror. I was happiest when I was out with my horse, galloping across the fields, putting as much distance as possible between myself and my father.

Chapter Twelve

BACK AT home, as I settled into the new school, my father settled into a new regime of torture.

One incident of sexual abuse became indistinguishable from the next, they all merged into one solid block of misery. The Nivea, the brown leather belt, the chilling death threats, all had a regular role in his perverted routine.

My own props were fantastical. *Tom and Jerry*, my outer body experiences, the separation of myself into two children. I developed a sort of steely fragility and coped the best way I could, knowing what was coming each time, yet powerless to stop it. But one day, when I was around 12, my father made a drastic change which would, even after everything I'd endured, leave me shell-shocked and scarred.

It started, as expected, with the dreaded signal of his head, and with it my throat constricted. Something shrivelled inside me. Since he had dragged me off the sofa by my ponytail, a couple of years earlier, I had never dared to disobey him again. The moment he tilted his chin, I scurried into my bedroom. He made an unfunny joke about what a fast runner I was and cackled with laughter. This was his warped version of being nice to me, it was the nearest I ever got to a compliment from him, and it only signalled that there was an attack just moments away. Dad's smile was like an air-raid siren. He only ever tried to be nice in the moments preceding the abuse. He was not so much Jekyll and Hyde. He was more Hyde and Double Hyde.

"Sit down on the edge of the bed," he ordered. "Now lie back."

I closed my eyes, summoning *Tom and Jerry* to my aid. I wanted to watch the episode where they both joined forces to rescue a baby, I needed to concentrate. I braced myself for the expected discomfort but instead, I heard the rustling of a bag. It completely threw me off track and my cartoon fizzled away. When I opened my eyes again, Dad was holding what looked like the handle of a spade. One edge had been rubbed down, so that it was smooth, but the other side was full of rough edges and splinters. I was perplexed. What, I wondered, had happened to the spade, and why was it in my room? Perhaps this wasn't what I had feared after all. Maybe he had no intention of attacking me. From the bag, Dad took a small tub of clear jelly and began rubbing it on the spade handle. And in that moment of sickening realisation, like a punch to the gut, I understood. I understood exactly.

"Please, Dad, No," I gasped. "Don't, please."

"Don't be so silly, it won't hurt," Dad replied, as though I was waiting for a routine vaccination.

"It will," I protested, staring at the flakes of wood on the rough side. "It will!"

When it came, the pain blowtorched right through my body. Dad shoved it in and out, faster and faster, until my agony consumed me. I could not breathe. I didn't want to breathe. I thought again of Bugsy and him being frightened to death. Could I die from pain? Was it possible? *Please*, I begged, *Let it be possible*. When eventually he took the handle out, I was raw and sore and felt sure I was bleeding down below. Dad, unconcerned, reached back into the bag and this time, produced a banana.

"No," I sobbed. "I can't take any more. Please don't, please."

I was wailing now, not caring who heard me or what the consequences were. I had been teetering at the very edge of what I could take, and now I had been tipped over.

"It's a banana!" Dad announced, as though I was over-reacting ridiculously. "It won't hurt at all."

But he was wrong. He pinned me down and thrust it back and forth, with such aggression, I felt as though I was being torn in two and quite possibly, I was. When it was over, he tossed it back into the bag. "Now, go and clean yourself up. And if you tell anyone, I will get my gun and I will kill you all," he said.

"Yes, please," I wept. "Please just kill me."

He turned on his heel and left, and I staggered into the bathroom and held a cold facecloth between my legs, it was all I could think of to ease the blistering pain, yet it was of no real use.

Crouching on the floor by the bath, I felt utterly desolate. I no longer cared if Dad shot me. It didn't matter. In many ways, I would have welcomed it. But I could not bear the thought of him shooting my mother too, I could not be responsible for her death. She had done nothing to deserve that. Yet at the same time, I harboured a growing anger and resentment towards her. Why did she never help me, or take my side? Why did she never ask me what was wrong?

I packaged the abuse away, I shrugged it off, I handed my burden over to another, imaginary child. Surely my own mother must have had some sense of what I was going through. My father was a devil and an ogre. I expected nothing from him as a parent, and I got even less. Yet rightly, or wrongly, I hoped for more from my mother. Paradoxically, I wanted to save her, but I also wanted her to save me. It breaks my heart still that she was not there for me when I needed her the most.

"Just kill me," I sobbed again, as I lay in the bathroom.

But there was nobody listening. Nobody to confide in about the abuse, nobody to even put me out of my misery. I knew dogs were not left to suffer like this. After the attack with the spade handle, my father left me alone for a while. I think perhaps he was afraid he had injured me, and it might have repercussions for him. Or it could be he was wary of pushing me too far in case I broke down and his secrets spilled out. There is also the third possibility that the abuse did in fact continue and I have blanked it out. I could not allow myself to endure any further abuse, and so I refuse to remember it. I will never know the truth of what really happened in those months that followed.

As I slowly healed down below, I spent hour after hour

lying in bed, thinking about Nan's embossed wallpaper and the deflated dots. There was no life left in them and there was no life left in me. My next clear memory is seared onto my brain and scrawled across my soul. I will never forget it. Nor do I think I will ever fully recover from it. Arriving home from school one afternoon, I ran straight from the car as usual to the stables, to see Fire.

"It's me!" I announced, as I banged open the wooden door.

But there was no welcoming whinny, no excited stamping of hooves. His stall was empty. In confusion, I ran back out to the yard.

"Is Fire in the field?" I asked Dad. "He's not in the stable."

There was a momentary pause, before he replied. And in that pause, my world shifted and slipped beneath me. In that pause, my world cracked, and shattered, and fell in upon me. That pause was everything.

"Sold him," he said, throwing his car keys into the air, and catching them again. "He's gone."

"Gone?" I repeated, the shock shooting through me like electric. Anger reared inside me, and in my mind's eye I saw Fire kicking up on his two back legs in protest. I loathed my father with every cell in my body, hated him on behalf of myself and even more, of Fire too. But I knew enough by now not to challenge him. I didn't say another word. I limped into the house, bone-weary and beaten. Fire was gone. My beloved friend, my saviour, was gone. And I did not even get to say goodbye.

As the days passed, the loss of my horse chafed and blistered, like an open wound. I had not thought my heart could weigh any heavier, but I was wrong. I spent every moment grieving for him and wept when I realised that I didn't have a photo to remember him by. I wondered how he was, if he was being well-treated, if his new owners, whoever they were, knew how much he liked to have his tummy tickled. I wondered if he missed me too.

"I love you, Fire," I said softly.

He had been more than a pet. He had stretched my horizons, socially, emotionally. He had been a crutch, a counsellor, a best pal. He had taught me so much more than simply how to ride.

Chapter Thirteen

NOT LONG after Fire was sold, we were on the move again, this time to a new home in Meare, Glastonbury.

The new house, inexplicably, was almost an hour away, and I had to move school again, find new friends, make yet another new start. But none of that really mattered. I just wanted to see Fire again. The move was my father's decision, to once again take me away from everything and everyone I knew. Perhaps he was getting edgy about the abuse, and he wanted to separate me from any friends I might confide in. More likely, he just enjoyed watching me struggle and suffer in a new environment. He seemed to get a sadistic pleasure simply from making up rules just for the hell of it.

At the new house, slowly unpacking my bags, I lined up my collection of Whimsies on my window, completely devoid of enthusiasm. I even had a miniature horse, a cruel reminder of Fire, and it pulled at my heartstrings as I placed it with the others.

Downstairs, Mum and Dad were arguing even more than usual. In the days before and after our move, they'd had terrible rows. It wasn't much of a secret that Dad had a girlfriend, called Steph, though nobody would have dared challenge him, least of all Mum. I suspected she had a boyfriend, too, though, as usual, she guarded her personal life very closely. My own soul-crushing turmoil continued – new house, same abuse. I gave up hope of it ever ending. After one attack, as Dad was fastening his belt, he nodded at my Whimsies on my windowsill, and said:

"If you open your mouth to anyone, I'll take all your Whimsies away, and then I'll kill you."

The words left me cold. In my child's mind, losing my Whimsies was of equal importance to me losing my life. I had so few possessions, so little that I held dear, and I treasured my tiny animals.

Another evening, I came home from school with a letter announcing a school disco.

"Can I go mum?" I asked. "Please?"

Mum was on her way out to work, running late, and preoccupied with trying to find her keys.

"I don't know, you're probably too young," she frowned distractedly, as she buttoned up her coat. "You should ask your father. It's up to him."

I baulked at the suggestion, and I had no intention of saying another word. But Dad had overheard from his office. "Yes, I don't see why not. I might have a fiver here for you, Sarah, if you play your cards right. That should cover it." He called.

His friendly tone was the red flag. I knew from bitter experience to be wary of my father when he was pretending to be nice. I heard him walking down the hallway and my stomach frothed and foamed like a rough sea. I thought I was going to be sick.

"It's OK," I stuttered. "I don't really want to…"

But Dad was towering over me now, his eyes darkening, his head slightly inclined. Without another word, I followed him to my bedroom, where he took what he felt was a suitable payment in kind.

"You keep this quiet, or I will kill you all," he told me – as usual, slapping a crisp five-pound note into my hand.

I went to the disco, as an escape from the house if nothing else. But my heart was no longer in it. Standing in the school hall, as the DJ belted out hits from the top 40, I felt so uncomfortable and ashamed, as though I didn't deserve to be there.

After I had paid for my ticket, I had change left to buy sweets and a drink. Such generosity was unheard of from my father and I should have made the most of it. But I had no appetite. There was a blockage in my throat, and I couldn't have swallowed a single thing. Instead, the coins scorched treacherously through my small hand. The attack had to be my fault, didn't it? I had asked for the money, after all. I was the one who had wanted a ticket for the disco. What would my teachers and classmates say if they knew what I'd done to pay for it?

The dull ache in my stomach and the stinging between my legs was reminder enough. The concepts of grooming and exploitation were beyond my years. And, aged 12, I blamed only myself. I felt judged and shamed and wretched.

The Letter

"You enjoy the disco then?" my father asked when I arrived home. "I'll take whatever change you've got left."

I did not want his money anyway. It was proof of my guilt.

"Thank you," I mumbled, tipping the money back into his palm.

We had only been living in the new house for around four or five months, when I went through a bout of sickness. I'd cooked sausages for tea the night before and picked up food poisoning. In the early hours, as I hung over the toilet bowl, Mum came in and said:

"You should have a day off school, tomorrow, Sarah, try and sleep it off."

Early the next morning, I was dimly aware of my siblings getting up and going downstairs for breakfast. Dozing off again, I was woken by a muffled argument behind my parents' bedroom door. I could only catch snatches of my mother's voice.

"Sarah certainly is not staying with you."

"Not as foolish as you think."

My pulse raced. Did my mother know? Was she confronting him about the sexual abuse? I could not be sure. But then I heard my father, his angry voice carrying right across the landing.

"Don't you dare ever speak to me like that!"

I heard my mother scream, and I vaulted out of bed and ran into their room. She was lying on the floor, curled into a ball, in a green dressing gown. Dad was already dressed for work, in his boots, kicking her in the face and in her side. I stood at the door, petrified, as his boot connected with her face again and again. Those boots suddenly seemed to be a savage metaphor for the way our house was run. Dad didn't allow any of us to wear shoes in the house. Yet he was allowed to wear his filthy work footwear and literally put the boot in on my mother. He aimed another kick at her ribs, before leaning down to wrap his hands around her neck. For a second, I was frozen with fear. But hearing her begin to choke, I snapped into action.

"Call the police!" I screamed over the bannister. "Dad is beating mum!"

Dad turned, his eyes black, spittle foaming around his lips.

"Get back to your room," he bawled.

His eyes met mine, and I like to think I matched him.

"Go to your room!" he ordered again, but I stood firm. I could not stand up for myself, but I would stand up for my mother. I would not leave her to be battered by him. He released his grip on her, shoved past me in the doorway and thundered down the stairs.

"Stephen!" he yelled.

Stephen, by now was aged 15, and had more or less left school, working full-time with my father as a builder. I huddled on the rug in the bedroom with Mum, both of us shivering like frightened little mice. I thought of *Tom and Jerry*, as I held her bruised hand in mine. I heard Dad grabbing his coat and opening the front door. His parting shot, when it came, was nothing if not predictable.

"Leave your mother where she is and if you call the police I will kill you."

Just to be sure, we stayed in the bedroom for ages, until

the sound of his van on the road had gone and we were confident it wasn't coming back.

"Help me get to the phonebox," Mum said.

Somehow, bloodied and bruised, she managed to make it to the nearby phonebox, and I called her friend's number as she instructed.

"From the sounds of it, you need to take your mum to the doctor," her friend said.

I was amazed nobody came to help, or even challenge us, as Mum limped along the road, leaning heavily into me, towards the doctors' surgery. It was morning rush hour, and the roads were busy. Yet everyone hurried past. It seemed people saw only what they chose to see.

"Leave your mother with me," said the GP. "I'll ensure she gets to hospital. You get yourself to school."

I nodded, but instead I went home and cleared away the breakfast dishes. All day, I was wracked with guilt. I couldn't be sure, but the snippets of argument I'd heard seemed to suggest Mum might suspect what Dad was doing to me. In that case, my childish logic told me it was my fault Dad had attacked her. I alone was responsible for her cuts and bruises. I had kept quiet for so long to try to keep my family safe. And now I had failed. Later in the day, I heard the bone-chilling sound of Dad's work van outside. I knew I had to face him and I was quaking with fear.

"Where's your mother?" he demanded, slamming in through the front door, as though all of this was someone else's fault.

"She's in the hospital," I replied quietly.

Dad glared at me and marched out again. It was a reprieve of some sorts, but I knew it was temporary. A couple of hours later, I heard his boots on the path outside again.

"They won't let me in!" he announced incredulously. "They won't let me in the hospital to speak to my own bloody wife!"

He expected me to share his outrage, but I said nothing. That night, as I was getting undressed upstairs, I heard his breath at my doorway. That was all it took, the sound of him breathing, and my whole body shuddered in protest. I followed him to his bedroom. "So, you be mum." He said.

On the outside, I betrayed very little. On the inside, my mind was racing, desperate for solutions. I looked at the window, could I jump right through it? There was a half-glass of water on the bedside table, could I smash it and cut my own throat? Could I drink the water and take all of Mum's tablets from her bedside drawer? Surely there was some way out of this. But Dad was already pulling back the duvet and so I climbed into Mum's side, next to the Nivea, her hairbrush, and a forgotten hair bobble. Lying next to him in the bed, our heads on adjoining pillows, was surreal and nauseating in equal measure. I was losing my grip on reality, unable any longer to distinguish between what was normal and what was grotesque.

"You open your mouth, you know what happens," Dad said, when he had finished.

I hurried back to my own bed, though I could not sleep at all.

Mum was in hospital for one week, and during that time, I took her place, in every single aspect. She did all the housework and chores, except for the shopping. My father had full control over all finances, and he didn't trust anyone else with the cash. He bought the food, and my mother was expected to cook it and clear it away. And so, each afternoon, after school, I did all her chores. I cooked and cleaned. I prepared packed lunches, I washed the dishes, I did the laundry and the ironing.

I cooked the same traditional meals as Mum would, lamb chops, boiled potatoes and peas; pie, mash and carrots; beef stew. And every night, after my work was done, I was expected to have sex with my father. My body was changing now, Dad had definitely noticed I had breasts and groped me during the assaults. But he never asked if I had my period yet and he made no mention of contraception or the risk of pregnancy. I never thought of it, I had so much else to worry about, and I would have been unable to raise the issue with him.

I was just 13 years old. My mother was in hospital. My father was sexually abusing me. My Nan was hundreds of miles away. Fire was gone. I had nobody. Not a soul on my side. I look back and do not know how my spirit did not crack completely.

Death would have been a kindness for me.

Chapter Fourteen

ON THE Friday of that week, I was sitting in class trying to ignore a nagging stomach cramp which had bothered me for a few days. Then, to my dismay, I felt a wet patch at the top of my legs, quickly spreading to the back of my skirt. My period had started, and it was so heavy I had to ask the teacher for help, and walk out of class, with my skirt stained a dark red. It was yet another mortifying incident to add to the many which had gone before it.

"Don't worry, we'll get you cleaned up in no time," smiled the school nurse. "It's unusual for a first period to be so heavy. I can't understand why you're bleeding so much."

I said nothing, but my mind was shuttering with snapshots from the brutal nightly attacks from my father. I had my own view on why my period had arrived now, and why it was so heavy. But again, all I felt was shame.

Two days later it was Sunday and by 11am, I had done the housework, and I was ready to start preparing the dinner. Dad and Stephen were at work, but I knew Dad would be expecting a full roast when he returned. I was busy peeling vegetables when my aunt suddenly appeared in the kitchen, red and flustered, with a roll of bin bags in her hand.

"Drop everything and pack what you need," she said. "You're leaving."

My eyes widened, first in shock and then, in glee.

"Come on!" she urged. "We need to get out of here before your father comes back. There isn't much time."

I left the half-peeled parsnip on the draining board and dried my hands. I was just opening out the first bin bag when the door opened again, and my mother shuffled in.

"I couldn't wait in the car," she said quietly. "I wanted to help."

Seeing her hobbling across the tiles, her arm in a sling, her face marbled with bruises, I felt again a pang of guilt. It was my fault she was in this state, I told myself.

"You sit here," I said, pulling out a dining chair. "I'll pack your stuff. Don't worry."

Mum sank into the chair, and I tried not to focus on the vivid purple lump above her eye which had forced it completely shut.

"Come on!" my aunt said. "Quickly! We don't want to be here when your dad gets back."

I buzzed around the house, from one room to another like an excited bumble bee, throwing clothes and essentials into bags.

"No knick-knacks, no luxury stuff," my aunt said firmly. "Just grab some clothes and off you go."

My gaze lingered on my precious line of Whimsies on the windowsill, I had spent years collecting them. But this was no time for sentimentality. I swept my clothes from the wardrobe into a bin bag and ran from my bedroom, leaving my little Whimsies staring after me. As I dragged my bulging bin bags down the stairs, I suddenly realised I didn't even know where we were going.

"We're going to Nan's, of course," Mum said.

"Hurray!" I yelled, and a real smile spread across my face for the first time in what felt like years.

Outside, a van was waiting to take us to Aberaeron. My aunt and I lugged a couple of mattresses down the stairs, along with blankets. With the van bursting with bin bags and bedding, we were ready to go. In less than an hour, we had packed up our lives and we were ready to leave for Nan's.

"On our way to Wales," I said softly to myself. "On our way to freedom."

I looked back at the house, the windows blank and unblinking, like all-seeing eyes, with no hint of the secrets they harboured. I thought of the tell-tale parsnip, half-peeled on the draining board, and envisaged my father's rage when he came home to discover we had gone. There was a pang of regret as I remembered Stephen, who we had left behind, because he was at work with Dad.

"Could we not have brought him along too?" I asked.

"It would have been too risky to wait for Stephen," Mum explained. "Stephen can join us if he wants to. I can come back for him next week."

Spotting the Severn Bridge and the pink castle held a certain nostalgia for me this time because I hoped this would be the last, for many months. I did not intend to ever come back to the place where I had suffered so much. It did not occur to me, on that journey, that I was escaping from the abuse. I focussed solely on keeping Mum and myself safe. Perhaps, also, I did not dare to even hope that it might one day end. I knew my father might track us down, might drag us back, might shoot us all. And so I was determined to enjoy this for what it was, a small smattering of happiness.

* * * *

At Nan's, we carried our belongings from home into the back downstairs room. Luckily, she had two living rooms, and we were given the use of an upstairs bedroom, too. She fussed over us, prepared us a little supper before bed, and made me feel as though this was just another holiday.

"We're going to love having you here," she smiled.

I had been at my new high school in Meare less than six months, and now, I was moving yet again. This time, it was not as difficult, because I remembered some of my class-mates from spending an academic year at the school, when I was 11. I met up with some old pals and settled in far more quickly than anyone expected.

I got a job, babysitting for a family who Nan knew, and spent all my wages on cassette tapes of my favourite bands, Madness, Abba and Boney M. I was a big Michael Jackson fan too. Together with my friends, I made up a dance routine for Brotherhood of Man's *Save All Your Kisses For Me*.

We'd meet up after school, hanging around the local bus shelter or we might ride our bikes down to a holiday park in the next village. We complained about our dismal maths lessons and swooned over the latest heartthrobs on *Top of The Pops*. For the first time in my life, I was beginning to feel like I was a normal girl. The weight of the abuse was there, always, like a rock rolling around in my stomach. But somehow, I learned to carry it. I reached a delicate balance to keep it from knocking around too much and causing damage.

The following summer, Gingerbread, a charity supporting single parent families, offered me a place on an Outward Bound holiday in the Welsh countryside.

"A holiday!" I exclaimed. "For me?"

It was my first ever holiday and I couldn't wait. I saved my babysitting wages for spending money, counting down the days on the calendar until we all went off in a battered old minibus. We stayed in a hostel, sleeping in one big dormitory. I loved it! There was a sense of camaraderie and together-ness, a feeling of family, without the threat I associated with being part of a family unit.

Each day we tried something new, abseiling, canoeing, rock-climbing. Exhilarated, I threw myself into each activity. On the last day, we went horse-riding. Tears pricked my eyes as I jumped up onto my horse and went into a gentle trot.

"You've obviously ridden a horse before," smiled the instructor. "Do you have your own?"

I shook my head, gulping back my sobs. On the journey back home, whilst everyone else sang songs, I thought only of Fire, and hoped he was well-loved. As much as I was trying to forget my childhood traumas, I knew I would never forget him.

At school, we had basic lessons in sexual education, with discussions on consent and abuse. They only confirmed that what Dad had done to me was neither normal, nor legal. In my heart, I'd suspected from the start that it was wrong. But over the years, the pieces had slowly slotted together like a ghastly jigsaw. The realisation of what my father was inched slowly around my body like ivy, threatening to choke me as it grew tighter and tighter. *A monster. A paedophile. A rapist.* Yet still, I kept quiet. I dared not speak out. Though Dad was out of my life, his threats rang crystal clear in my head, as though they had been made yesterday.

"Open your mouth and I will kill you."

A few months on, Mum was allocated a council house, close to Nan's. Though I would rather have stayed with Nan, it was still a happy time. Mum seemed to have relaxed and softened significantly since leaving Dad, I told myself it was the Welsh effect, the sea air was good for everyone. One night, as I was drifting off to sleep, she came in and cupped my cheek with her hand.

"I love you, Sarah," she told me softly.

I couldn't remember her ever telling me she loved me before, and to my embarrassment, I felt tears streaming down my cheeks. They were the words I'd longed to hear from her, and now my emotions spilled over.

"Love you too," I mumbled.

Other times, she began giving me a quick squeeze as I was on my way out to school, or she'd snuggle up on the sofa in the evenings as we watched TV. Often, she was at work when I came home, and there was usually a meal prepared and waiting to go in the oven. Previously, her notes had been very factual: *Heat for one hour at 150.* Now, she was light-hearted and affectionate: *Hope you've had a good day, heat this through at 200. Love you lots, Mum.* I welcomed this new version of Mum, and I was thirsty for more. She was letting her guard down. Better still, she was inviting me in. And she even became a little more open about her past. She admitted Dad had hit her previously, before the attack in Meare, and on one occasion in October 1971, she was so frightened she had run away. I was later taken into foster care, aged two, because there was nobody left to look after me.

"How long did you run away for?" I asked curiously. "Why did I need to go into care? Why did you not come back?"

And the obvious question, which I could not say out loud, because I was frightened of the reply: *Why did you not take me with you?*

But Mum's defence was up again, like an automatic barrier. I sensed she already felt she had said too much, and she refused to share any more details. Years later, when I obtained copies of my social services records, I came across a newspaper cutting headed: *Mother Of Two is Missing.* Open-mouthed, I read that our neighbours had reported a disturbance, after which Mum had vanished for days. I was taken into foster care until she was found. But, after all that, she still went back to my father. It was a decision I found hard to understand and yet I also appreciated that he had controlled her, perhaps with the same threats he used to control me.

I wished so much, as our bond strengthened, that I could ask her about the abuse. If she knew, what she knew, and crucially, if she could help me. But Dad's tried and tested fury was stronger than Mum's fledgling kindness, and I could not take that risk.

Chapter Fifteen

NOT LONG after we moved into the new house, Mum introduced me to her new partner, Chris. They had been friends for some time. Chris seemed like a nice bloke, he was nothing like my father. And yet, right from the start, I pushed against him joining our family.

I was wary of men and of father figures in particular. I felt uncomfortable around him, on edge, and always waiting for an aggression or a perversion to leak out from under his smiling facade. It was all I had ever known, and I expected it was only a matter of time for Chris to be unveiled as a monster, just like my father. I did not want him in our family. I could not take that risk. Yet there was an element of self-interest too. I had got used to having Mum to myself, and I felt like I was just getting to know this softer, gentler side to her. A nascent bond was forming between us, thin and fragile, but it was there all the same. Now, with Chris on the scene, I felt side-lined, as though I had fallen down her list of priorities, once again.

To me, aged 14, he was ruining everything. He was just

another man who had bludgeoned his way into my life, to make me feel bad. I am ashamed to admit it, but I was not very nice to Chris at all in those early days.

"You're not my Dad," I told him scathingly. "So don't start trying to act like it."

I didn't do anything he asked, I played him and Mum off against each other, and I was rude and sulky. I made his life as awkward as possible, hoping, I suppose, that he wouldn't stick around. Yet, as the months went on, and he tolerated my outbursts without retaliation, I developed a genuine respect for him, and I slowly accepted that he was here to stay.

I also saw how content Mum was with him, and again, my emotions were split. Part of me wanted her to be happy. But I also begrudged it. I felt let down by her, all over again and, as usual, she either couldn't or wouldn't see it. The obvious advantage of her seeing Chris was there was no chance of my father steaming back in, which gave our lives some stability. I never wanted to see him again. But one day, I got home from school to find Mum sitting at the kitchen table with a letter.

"We have to go to court," she told me. "You need to decide who you would like to live with, me or your father."

Just the sound of his name, in conjunction with my living arrangements, sent an icy chill through me.

"I want to stay with you, please," I said quietly, and she smiled.

"It'll be OK," she replied, and squeezed my hand.

The trip to Somerset, for the court hearing, was memorable mainly because I was allowed a day off school. I had a very brief conversation with a social worker, who asked me where I would like to live, and then we drove home again. On the journey back to Wales, I felt myself sagging with relief. I believed that was the end of it. But just a few days later, another letter arrived.

"Your father has been granted access," Mum said, wearily. "He's coming to visit next weekend."

I was on my way out to school and, suddenly unsteady on my legs, I dropped my bag and stumbled onto a chair.

"I don't want to see him," I said, covering my face with my hands. "Please don't make me."

Mum sighed.

"It's not up to me," she said. "The courts have made a decision, and you have to do as you're told."

The following Saturday I was in my bedroom, gnawing at my fingernails, when the doorbell rang.

"Sarah!" my mother called.

I was shaking as I made my way down the stairs, my skin tingling with anxiety. I was terrified of seeing my father again.

"Well, aren't you quite the young lady now," he said, with his reptilian grin.

In his van, I felt horribly exposed, as though I didn't have enough clothing on, even though I was rugged up in my jeans and coat. I huddled up, right against the door, as far away from him as I could get.

"I'm going to see one of my mates off the radio," Dad said, as he turned into a side street. "You wait here. Won't be long."

And that was how it went. He used his time with me to visit people he'd met on Ham radio, trekking across the country and leaving me in the van for hours while he socialised.

Aged 14, I could not understand why he bothered with me at all. He certainly had no interest in being a father. He barely spoke to me, and he didn't plan anything for me. As an adult, I now realise he was keeping tabs on me, making sure I was still frightened of him, checking I hadn't been tempted to share my secret. Those visits were all about him keeping me in my box.

The access continued, maybe once a month, and Dad began work on a relative's building extension. He was staying over so he could get the job done more quickly, and I began visiting him there instead. Those visits were much less intimidating, because I was surrounded by relatives. But one day when we arrived, the place was empty. Everyone was out. We walked into the tiny hallway and, as I raised my head, I saw Dad's eyes darken and his chin tilted. It was as though all my insides had fallen out, into a big messy puddle beneath me. I felt like there was nothing holding me together.

"Here," he said, pushing open the door to the room where he was sleeping.

Every bone in my body screamed out against it. But I had no choice. When it was over, he drove me back home, just as if nothing had happened.

"You remember what I said," he snarled, as I climbed out of the van. "I've still got my guns. You tell anyone and I will shoot the lot of you."

It was as though he had raped me simply to remind me

what was at stake. To refresh my memory of his wickedness. As the shock settled, however, I was filled with a growing defiance. I would not disobey him, I could not put my family at risk. But instead, I could make sure it never happened again. Now I was a bit older, and there had been a period of time between the attacks, I had more clarity and more purpose. Maybe I had a smidgeon more confidence too.

"I don't want to see Dad again," I told Mum. "I'm not going next time."

She shrugged, distracted, as always, with something more important.

"Well, you'll have to explain yourself to the social worker I suppose," she said, after I repeated my statement. "I'm not getting involved."

That could have been her mantra throughout life. She just did not want to get involved. The day after the latest rape, I pulled on my coat and knocked on every shop, pub, and café in the village, asking for work. As it happened, *The Prince Of Wales*, the pub where my mother already worked, was looking for kitchen help at weekends.

"When can you start?" asked the landlord.

"Immediately," I replied. "And I can work every weekend too."

Mum was pleased I'd got a job, she was glad I'd be earning my own money. And the fact that my working hours clashed with Dad's visits didn't seem to occur to her.

"Can't see him," I said, when the next visit rolled around. "I'm working all weekend."

And that was my way out. My job at the pub put a stop

to my time with my father, and to his abuse, and nobody challenged it or even questioned why I did not want to see him. The adults, the social workers, the court representatives, did nothing. It was left to me to keep myself safe in the end. And as it turned out, I loved my new job. I met more friends, kitchen staff like me, and when we weren't working, we'd hang around the village, swapping gossip and listening to music from the charts on a ghetto blaster.

There was one boy who really seemed to like me, but I didn't for a minute think it was anything sexual. In my mind, I was damaged goods. I couldn't think why anyone would ever be interested in me. We spent lots of time together, yet each time he tried to get close, I pulled back. When he paid me compliments, I became distant and off-hand, making excuses for us not to be alone together.

Comparisons with my mother were inevitable, if only from myself. It was frustrating that I was making the same mistakes as her, and yet I couldn't help it. Any close friendships, any intimacy, scared me and I retreated further and further into the safety of my shell. I was stubborn too; inflexible and obstinate, just like her. And so though I wanted to change, I refused to do so. Part of me liked the similarities, she was my mother, after all. I hoped in vain that these shared traits might foster a closer bond between us. But I was afraid, also, of ending up like her.

By my 15th birthday, in April 1984, I was earning a steady wage at the pub and managing to put a little by in my savings each week. I needed transport to get to and from work, especially late at night, and so, I decided I would sell my flute and buy myself a scooter, using the proceeds and my savings. The dreaded flute, synonymous with the abuse, had been sitting in the fancy velvet case, untouched, for years. Somehow, I felt I'd earned that flute by having sex with my father, and I could not bear to even look at it. The flute itself, in my mind, had colluded with my father. It was a form of blackmail, all part of the package.

"If you tell anyone what has happened, I will take away your new flute. Then I will take my gun from my office, and I will shoot you all."

"Give it a good clean and you'll get a better price for it," Mum suggested.

When I opened the case, the silver caught the light and glinted mockingly at me. In an instant, time unravelled back to that Christmas night, the darkness, the fear, the rough beard on my face, the hand over my mouth, the smell of cigars. Each memory overlaid the next until I clasped my hands over my eyes, unable to take any more. With my trademark shrug, I threw my memories back into the past, and gave the flute one last polish. As I snapped the lid closed, I breathed a sigh of relief. I would be glad to see the back of it.

I placed an ad in the window of the local shop and got a good price for it, enough to buy myself a secondhand blue 50cc Honda. I loved my little scooter, the freedom it gave me and the adventures I had. I visited pals in nearby villages, I went riding along the coast and out through the countryside. Flying down the country lanes, the wind whipping back my hair, I couldn't help thinking of my beloved Fire. The sound of his low whinny and his stamping hooves echoed through my mind. I pictured his nose and mouth, puckering up for a kiss. I wondered again where he was and if he was loved.

"I'm sorry, Fire," I said softly. "You deserved much better."

I did not see it then, but I deserved much better, too.

Chapter Sixteen

ONE SATURDAY evening, after a long shift at the pub, I came home to find my brother, Stephen, in the living room.

"When did you get here?" I asked, my face splitting into a big beam.

We were not an affectionate family, so there was no hug, not even a handshake. But I was quietly pleased to see him. I hadn't seen Stephen since we'd left Meare, and I had missed him.

"Dad's working round here, he dropped me off on his way past," Stephen explained. "I'm going to stay for a while. Mum says it's OK."

I was looking forward to us spending some time together. Now 17, Stephen had grown to look very much like Dad, so much that the resemblance was quite startling. Stephen was slimmer than Dad, and his eyes were blue, instead of Dad's dark brown. But apart from that, they looked very similar. Anxiously, I pushed the thought away. Looks, I reminded myself, were superficial. They might look alike, but they were two distinct and different individuals.

The Letter

Stephen and Dad shared the same first name too, they were both called Arthur, Dad was Arthur William, my brother was Arthur Stephen. It was a reflection, no doubt, of Dad's swollen ego and his determination to control every aspect of his family that he had saddled his eldest son with the same name as himself. My paternal grandfather was also called Arthur; it was a pattern which might, within a different narrative, have been an endearing family tradition. To me, it showed itself as a toxic thread, running through the male side of the family and my father, misogynistic and twisted, had seized upon it. But I reassured myself again, none of this was Stephen's fault. He couldn't help looking like his father nor had he any say in the name he was given.

As a child, he had witnessed Dad's physical violence, and lived in fear of him, as I had. He was a victim of the violence, just like me.

They're not the same people, I told myself again.

That first evening, it was great to catch up. Stephen had been living and working full-time with Dad, but announced he'd had enough.

"I just need a break," he told me. "From the job and from Dad."

He didn't mention Dad's temper, but he didn't need to.

"It'll be nice to have you around," I grinned.

But the next morning, when I wandered into the kitchen in my dressing gown, Stephen said:

"I think we need to lay down a few ground rules here. For a start, you should have been up earlier, getting breakfast ready."

I stared incredulously, wondering whether he was joking. But there was no hint of a smile.

"Stephen, you sound just like Dad," I spluttered. "You can't walk in and start shouting the odds. This isn't even your house."

He stalked out, slamming the kitchen door, and my heart sank. What had happened to him? Later, I heard him arguing with Mum because his dinner wasn't ready on time.

And when I left for work, early evening, he confronted me again.

"I want to know what time you're going to be in tonight," he demanded. "You need some discipline. Ground rules, like I said."

I recoiled. It was as if, for some strange reason, he was modelling himself on Dad. Yet as far as I knew, he loathed Dad and was just as wary of him as I was. So why would he want to be like him? Had they spent so much time together that Stephen had subconsciously adopted his bullying ways?

"I mean it," Stephen glowered.

"Look," I reasoned. "I don't need to answer to you, you're my brother. You're only two years older than me, for goodness' sake. And stop moaning at Mum as well. We've managed perfectly well without you for two years. We don't need you turning up with your stupid rules and ruining it all. We're happy here, you know."

As I made my way down the path, I felt his eyes boring through me from the doorway. And late that night, when I arrived home, he was waiting with a face like thunder.

The Letter

"You're 15," he snarled. "You should be home in bed, not riding round on a bloody scooter."

"None of your business," I quipped before hurrying upstairs, sounding braver than I felt.

For deep down, I was unnerved.

His behaviour shocked and unsettled me in equal measure. I wondered again about Dad's decision to give Stephen his own name. I worried it reflected an ominous determination to mould his son into a new version of himself.

* * * *

A couple of weeks later, I arrived back from school on the bus as usual. It was around 4pm, and Mum had gone to work but had left a casserole under some foil with a note on the kitchen table.

"Heat this for around 40 minutes," I read out loud. "Bring washing in please. Love Mum."

I switched the oven on to warm up and then ran upstairs to get changed out of my uniform. I was just stepping out of my school skirt when my bedroom door opened, and Stephen barged into my room.

"Hey!" I began. "I'm just getting cha —"

Before I could turn to face him, he had grabbed me, thrown me onto my bed and flipped me over. I was trussed up, with my legs somehow twisted underneath me, so that I was pinned in place. With Stephen's weight on me, I might as well have been stapled to the duvet. It all seemed to happen in one swift, alarming move. Without speaking, he pulled my underwear to the side and raped me. It was over so fast, and I was so stunned, I did not once cry out. I did not even struggle. I could not believe it had happened. I felt like I had dropped into a parallel universe, fallen into the middle of a horror film, similar to the way in which I used to teleport into the world of *Tom and Jerry* – except this time, it was the reverse effect. The alternate reality was truly horrific.

"If you tell anyone about this, I'll say you wanted it," Stephen hissed.

The words were like an ice-pick right through the side of my skull. What would people think of me; a girl who *wanted* sex with her own brother? Stephen smiled salaciously and then he was gone.

After I heard him stomping noisily across the landing, I ran into the bathroom and grabbed Mum's paracetamol. With trembling fingers, I emptied the packet into my hand. My mind was on fast forward, whirling, swirling, as though I was caught in a blizzard. I could not open the blister packs fast enough, I could not wait to be dead. I was in such a hurry to rid my mind of what I had just endured. I swallowed the lot with a cupful of tap water and ran back to my room, impatiently waiting to fall unconscious.

Let me be dead, let me be dead, let me be dead.

For hours, I lay on my bed, images lapping at the edge of my mind. Dad looming over me in the caravan, the Nivea tub in his hand. Dad raping me in his bedroom.

"You be mum."

Dad unbuckling his belt; that gentle clink, loaded with metallic menace.

The Letter

"You open your mouth and I will kill you. I will shoot you all."

And now Stephen too. What was so fundamentally wrong with me that my Dad and my brother both felt I was fair game? It had to be my fault. It just had to be. Had I encouraged them in some subconscious way? Had they plotted this together? Perhaps Stephen was raping me on Dad's behalf, as punishment for me refusing to see him again?

Stephen's betrayal hurt equally but differently. I couldn't remember a time I had ever trusted my father, I had grown up terrified of him. But as children, Stephen and I had been close. I had trusted him, liked him, loved him as a big brother. How had it all gone so wrong?

Desperately, so desperately, I needed these evil thoughts to stop. Quite simply, I needed to die. As it grew dark, my head pounded, but I remained stubbornly conscious. I had saved all my wages to buy a pink duvet cover which I'd wanted for months. As my tears flowed and soaked it through, I wondered what the point was – of the new duvet, of anything at all. Every time I tried to move on with my life, each time I stumbled across a small pocket of happiness, it was brutally snuffed out by my own family. Why? I pulled at the pink duvet, trying and failing to rip it to pieces with my bare hands. I thought of Nan's wallpaper, the bubbles which I had popped, one by one. And again, I understood that all of this was wrong. So wrong.

Suddenly claustrophobic and anxious to be out of the house, I jumped up and ran downstairs. I sat in the bus shelter on my own, my head whirring and my body aching, until it grew so late that I knew Mum would be fretting about me.

"Why didn't you have the casserole?" she asked when I finally staggered back inside. "The oven was on when I got home, but you forgot to put the casserole in."

"Not hungry," I mumbled.

"Well," she humphed. "That's gratitude for you. You didn't even bring the washing in, it's still on the line and it's gone damp now."

The next day, Stephen was perfectly civil with me, as though nothing at all had happened. He continued trying to enforce new house rules, dictating when I should be home and what chores I should do. But he made no mention of the attack, and neither did I. There was no friendship between us, no bond, but neither was there any obvious discord. I was living in a pressure cooker, with immense stress and tension hissing and bubbling beneath the surface. It took all of my strength and self-control to keep it from boiling over.

"I don't know what's the matter with you two," Mum said, nodding at Stephen and me. "You both have a face like a wet weekend. Why don't you go out together, to the cinema or something?"

I could not credit that she couldn't sense the unease. It was so potent, so heavy, I could almost taste it. The air was thick with it. Yet, as always, Mum bypassed it without a second glance. She didn't like to look too deeply into anything. Perhaps she suspected she might not like what she found.

"Sibling rivalry," she sighed eventually, when neither of us spoke. "That's all it is."

Chapter Seventeen

LATER THAT same year, Mum and her boyfriend, Chris, moved to a new home in the same village, a lovely double fronted house with big rooms and more space.

Stephen came with us.

He seemed to be back home permanently now. He'd had no job for a while after moving back and so Mum and Chris bought him a motorbike, to help him search for work. He'd got a job working with an electrician but was sacked soon after, because he was always oversleeping and turning up late. Now, he was back on the dole and itching to cause trouble in all the spare time he had.

Nobody mentioned the glaring irony of him insisting on laying down rules for everyone else, yet not following any himself. I could not help thinking of my father and his 'no shoes in the house' rule. We all walked about in socks whilst Dad marched up and down in his work boots. And now Stephen handed out tasks whilst doing precisely nothing himself. I recalled again the physical similarities between them and their shared name. Fretfully, I pushed my worries away, but they hung, like cobwebs, in the dusty corners of my mind.

At the new house I had a bedroom of my own and soon settled in with my pink duvet cover on my bed and my Michael Jackson posters on the walls. One Friday evening, I was home alone. Friday was always the night for the supermarket shop and Mum and Chris liked to go together. I'd had a bath, and had a towel around me, ready to get into my pyjamas, when I heard a noise on the landing. I stiffened. I hadn't heard Stephen come in, maybe he'd been here all along. Before I could push a chair up against the bedroom door, it was flung open, and there he was. I was petrified. It was going to happen again, I knew it, and there was absolutely nothing I could do to stop it.

Like Dad, Stephen seemed to have a preferred routine and the second rape was almost a carbon copy of the first. He dragged my towel away, flipped me over and rammed my head into the bed. Though only two years older he was much bigger and stronger than me. I might as well have been a small ladybug, crushed in the palm of his sticky hand. My pink duvet had slipped off the bed in the struggle and my face was pressed so hard into the white sheet, I feared I might suffocate. I couldn't breathe. My chest was bursting, and my head was throbbing. Afterwards, he said again:

"You breathe a word, I'll tell everyone you asked for it. I'll tell them you *wanted* it."

He lingered on the words, savouring them, almost as though the idea amused him, as though he was proud of the threat he'd concocted. When he had gone, I locked myself in the bathroom and switched the shower onto the hottest setting. Again, I was tormented by thoughts which buzzed around my head like angry bluebottles. I needed them to stop. The hot water scalded me as I scrubbed and scrubbed. I was red raw and sore, but I continued to scour my skin like it was a dirty pan. And yet still, as I stepped out of the shower, into the steam of the bathroom, I felt I was crawling with a thousand tiny insects. I was dirty and disgusting. Weak and worthless. Why hadn't I fought back? Why hadn't I screamed out? I was angry with myself, furious at my own passivity. What was wrong with me?

In anguish I opened the bathroom cabinet and emptied out all Mum's tablets, painkillers, antihistamines, stomach settlers – anything I could find. I was determined to finish the job this time. I swallowed the lot in a few mouthfuls, hoping for any kind of relief.

As I stumbled from the bathroom, back to my bedroom, I spotted Stephen, through his open bedroom door, lying on his bed. He was stretched out, feet crossed, hands behind his head. So relaxed, he might as well have been sunbathing. It defied all belief. He had no remorse, no grasp of the magnitude of suffering he had inflicted on his own sister. He looked, if anything, quite content. Wedging my bedroom door shut, I curled up on my bed in despair, childhood memories of Stephen flickering in and out of my consciousness; Stephen showing me my coat peg on my first day at school, Stephen carrying me over a stream in the woods when it got too deep, Stephen blowing up my floats before we swam in the outdoor pool at the big house. How had he gone from that – to this? I heard Mum arriving home, and the rustle of bags as she unloaded the shopping from the car.

"Sarah!" she called. "Could you give me a hand down here please?"

As I swung my legs wearily over the bed, I felt a sharp pain behind my eyeballs and a tide of vomit rushed up my throat. Dashing to the bathroom, I was violently sick.

"What's the matter?" Mum asked, coming in behind me.

The empty blister packs of tablets were on the bathroom floor, but she seemed not to notice them.

"Have you got food poisoning?" she asked. "Or a tummy bug? What is it now?"

All I heard, in my anguish, was "now" as though this was just the latest in a long, disappointing list of transgressions. Maybe my own mother thought it was all my fault too.

"Sarah?" she prompted. "I'm waiting for an answer."

In between sobs, I mumbled I was just feeling unwell and stressed.

"I'll get a shower," I said, wiping my mouth with a tissue. "Maybe I'll feel better then."

"Good idea," Mum replied.

After the shower, aside from a headache, I didn't even feel sleepy. I was so frustrated at my own inadequacy. Why couldn't I just kill myself? Why was I so bad at everything? When I was in bed, late in the evening, Mum came in and perched awkwardly on the end of the duvet.

"I brought you a glass of water," she said. "Are you feeling better? What are you stressed about?"

It was the first time she'd ever asked me a direct question

and it floored me. Did she really want an honest answer? Did she actually want to know? Yet I could not confide in her about Stephen without it spilling out about Dad too. I had the feeling that once I started, I wouldn't be able to stop. That by telling the truth I would be detonating a bomb which might well kill us all.

"I will shoot you and I will shoot your mother."

Staring at my ruined fingernails, I took in a deep breath and said:

"Oh, you know, teenage stuff, nothing major."

It was evidently the reply she'd hoped for, and she patted my duvet in satisfaction before getting up to leave. Again, I was more like my mother than I cared to admit. When it came to the crunch, I just couldn't do it. I dared not open my mouth. The difference, of course, was that I was a child, and she was an adult. I was being threatened and bullied and abused. But I did not see any of that. I saw only that I had failed.

* * * *

The day after the rape, it was as if nothing had happened.

At breakfast, Stephen was just the same as ever; cold but civil. He didn't make conversation but neither did he go out of his way to ignore me. It was as if, like my father, he didn't believe, or didn't want to believe, he'd done anything wrong. And whilst, inwardly, I recoiled every time his sleeve brushed mine, or he pinched a slice of toast off my plate, I also tried to continue with the usual routine. I didn't want anyone to find out what he had done to me, least of all my own family.

"I'll tell people that you wanted it…"

The crippling cloud of shame was far greater than any desire I might have had to unburden myself. I did my best to avoid being in the house alone with Stephen, and there were many occasions when I went out to meet my friends, or I simply walked alone around the village, instead of risking being in the house on my own with him. A couple of weeks later, though, I arrived back from school and was confronted by Stephen in the hallway.

"Hello," I said warily, instantly on edge.

I was suddenly horribly aware of how vulnerable I was, conscious of my bare legs underneath my skirt, mindful of his bulk towering over me. I dashed upstairs, but he followed and shoved his way into my room, quickly closing the door behind us. He must have noticed me shaking because he laughed scornfully.

"Stop panicking, I'm not going anywhere near you," he said.

That in itself felt, perversely, like an insult and a rejection. I did not want Stephen anywhere near me. But neither did I like him treating me like a virus, which was exactly how he was behaving.

"You might have an STD," he began.

I looked at him, uncomprehending.

"A sexually transmitted disease," he said impatiently. "I've picked something up from a girl I slept with. You need to check yourself. But don't go to the GP, they might ask questions. Remember, you need to keep quiet, or I'll tell everyone how much you wanted it."

The beginnings of a smile played around his lips and my stomach somersaulted. Retching, I threw myself onto my duvet. I didn't know what an STD looked like, but as far as I knew I was clear, for now. Every morning, in addition to worrying Stephen might attack me, I now panicked I had contracted a terrible illness too.

The weeks passed, and I had no symptoms at all. But the sickness in the pit of my stomach remained. Stephen left me completely alone, maybe he was worried about passing on the infection, and me reporting him to a doctor. Or perhaps there was simply no opportunity; I had thwarted his plans by making sure I was always busy with school, my job and my friends.

"You're hardly at home these days," Mum commented. "I never see you!"

"I'm just working hard, saving up," I replied. "That's all."

Several times, after my shower before bed, she'd express her amazement at the steam in the bathroom.

"Why do you have the water so hot?" she asked. "You'll burn yourself, Sarah."

One evening, I ran a bath instead, and Mum dipped her hand in while I was getting my nightclothes ready.

"This water is scalding," she exclaimed. "It will cost a fortune to heat the water to this temperature and it can't be good for you. I don't understand how you can enjoy a boiling hot bath."

How could I tell her it was not about enjoyment, it was

about cleansing, purging and ridding myself of the filth imbued in me by my father and brother. It was a habit which continued right through adulthood. I always wash, even today, under the hottest possible setting. One day, I hope, I will walk out of the bathroom and feel truly cleanI was almost 16 when, one weekend, I was asked to help out sorting through video tapes for a family friend who was opening a hire shop. I jumped at the chance of earning a few extra pounds, and also of keeping out of Stephen's way. But when I arrived at the shop, Stephen was there, in the back room, searching through piles of video cassette tapes.

"Thought I'd offer to help as well," he said, with a thin smile.

My mind was racing furiously. I couldn't think of a decent excuse to leave, and so I put my bag down and began categorising the tapes. He wouldn't try anything here, I told myself. Not in someone else's shop. It would be too risky, too exposed. I blinked away a brief reminder of the sexual assault in the horsebox, the rapes in the stables, the attack in the loft at the big house. Dad was perfectly at ease, carrying out his perversions in public. Why would Stephen be any different?

For a while, he was engrossed in the titles, and then, when he came across the one he had been searching for, he slotted it into a video player. By now, the shop owner had left and it was just Stephen and I left in the building. A pornographic film started to play, and Stephen glanced at me. His eyes were blue, nothing like Dad's, and yet in that moment, they were filled with the same lust, the same warped depravity.

"Sit down and watch it," he ordered.

My pulse galloping, I made for the door. But Stephen was too fast for me. He lunged for the handle, locked it and grabbed me. But this time, as he tried to flip me over, I managed to wriggle free. Like a wild cat, I began kicking and hitting, my arms and legs flailing, my eyes wide open with fear and protest.

"No!" I yelled. "Leave me alone! No!"

Perhaps Stephen was worried someone would hear me because he released his grip instantly. He dropped me and left, leaving the porn film still playing, a fitting backdrop to his sordid little plan. Sobbing, I sank like a ragdoll into a crumpled heap amongst the video tapes. I was frightened that I had angered him, I had defied him, and he would surely seek some sort of revenge. And yet deep down there was a kernel of hope, too. Because at last, I was fighting back. I had already taken a stand against my father, and now against my brother too. This was the uprising. This was me, letting them know I was wrestling back some control over my life. I was not beaten yet.

Chapter Eighteen

IN APRIL 1985, my 16th birthday came and went without much of a fuss. My mother bought me a small gift and, to my delight, suggested she take me to the local pub for a drink.

"I'll get you a Babycham," she said conspiratorially. "Nobody will know you're 16. My treat."

It felt rebellious, drinking in public for the first time. But I loved it, less for the risk, more for the connection I felt with my mother.

"I wish we could do this every week," I told her, as we ordered chips and another drink.

But she just laughed. To her, it was a throwaway comment. To me, it was baring my soul, pleading for her to hear my voice. The outing was lovely but as always, I wished for more from her. Talking to my mother was like pulling a thread, halfway, before it snapped. I never ever got to the end of it, never truly got to the real her.

"Happy Birthday, darling," she said absently, as we arrived home later in the evening.

There was nothing personal, nothing maternal, in her

words. I could not articulate what was missing, only that I felt the void so keenly.

The following day, I celebrated with my friends, out in the village on our scooters. I heard nothing from my father and had not expected to. He was not the type to remember a birthday, less still mark it in any way. I did not miss him, but I did miss the idea of a father. I longed for the type of dad my friends had, loving, protective and, above all, safe. Everything my own was not. And yet, I had my beloved Grandad, and my relationship with Chris was improving steadily. I had other male role models to be proud of. And so, on my milestone birthday, I tried to focus on what I had, and not what was lacking.

Two months on, I left school, and Stephen turned 18. He had been talking about throwing a party for months beforehand and my mother had eventually caved in and agreed. It seemed to me he got his way far more than I did. It grated on me that he was gifted a motorbike and yet I had bought my own scooter. My 16th birthday had passed quietly, and though I didn't want a party for myself, I wasn't offered one either.

Stephen had a way of getting my mother to agree to his demands. Perhaps she, like me, saw glimmers of my father in him and she did not dare defy him. For his party, she hired a room at the local holiday park, and plans began to celebrate his big day in style. Naturally, everyone presumed I would attend, and there was no good reason for me not to. Many of my friends and family would also be there, and so I went along, on the night, without really looking too deeply into how very wrong it all was.

I didn't buy Stephen a gift, or even a card. I don't remember wishing him a happy birthday. And yet I didn't even think about not showing up.

"Happy Birthday to you!" sang the guests, as Stephen took an exaggerated bow and accepted the gifts and the free drinks that followed.

Holding a lukewarm Babycham, I tried to sing, and I tried to smile. But the attacks bubbled and fizzed behind my fake grin. Snapshots of the rapes shot in and out of my mind like fireworks, vivid and fizzing one minute, black and smoky the next. I couldn't quite shake the memories, no matter how hard I pushed them down. Yet neither did I dare to speak out. The two threats ran parallel in my mind, each equally as effective as they were disparate:

"You open your mouth, I'll shoot you. I'll shoot the lot of you."

"You breathe a word, I'll tell everyone you wanted it. I'll say you loved it."

I looked around the party room, at the balloons, the cake, the egg butties. And I imagined Stephen grabbing the mic from the DJ and shouting:

"She wanted it you know! She really enjoyed it! My sister! Now you know what she's really like!"

The fear was so great it pinned me to the parquet. I stood, immobile, at the side of the dancefloor, my stomach heaving. Nobody would believe me. They would all believe him. Stephen was older than me. He was an adult. I was soiled goods, I was grubby, broken and lost. Why would anyone take me seriously?

Besides, as I watched Nan and Grandad dancing, and I saw

Mum beaming and chatting with relatives, I knew I could not land this on them. I could not launch this atom bomb into their lives. If I told them about Stephen, the abuse by Dad would also tumble out. The two were intertwined in my mind; connected in ways I would never truly know or understand. Not only would I shatter the family by sharing my secret, but I would also be putting their lives at risk. I had to keep quiet. It was the only way. And that was not all. For even then, even after the rapes, the violence, the scornful, gloating, threats, I clung still to a tiny scrap of sympathy for my brother. He'd also had a tough childhood with Dad's violence on one side and Mum's indifference on the other. I knew how lonely that felt. In my heart, I believed he was, in a sense, a victim. Or perhaps it was just less painful for me to see him in that way.

Later that same summer, I was in my bedroom, with the windows open, on a warm day. When Stephen appeared at my doorway, I didn't at first feel too alarmed. He had left me alone since the incident at the video shop, around six months earlier. I was fully dressed too, and I knew Mum and Chris were outside in the garden.

"What do you want?" I asked, avoiding eye contact.

Instead of replying, he walked towards me, and shoved me violently to the floor. All at once, my adrenalin kicked in.

Fight back, I reminded myself. *You can do it. Remember last time.*

As I fell backwards onto the carpet, I drew my legs up to kick him in the chest, which knocked him off balance for a second and gave me time to scramble out of the way.

"Leave me alone!" I screamed.

There was a moment of quiet – a moment of menace – as Stephen loomed over me, his blue eyes seeming suddenly dark, a trick of the light which transported me right back to my childhood. My imagination tore a gaping hole in time and space, and there I was, back in the caravan, with Dad standing over me, his dark eyes glittering, his belt clinking in warning.

"No!" I yelled again.

And this time, I was shouting at my father. My six-year-old self was kicking and biting and fighting for my life. All the hurt, all the pain of those years rushed out into the air and I was battling back against each and every time I had been violated. In the chaos, I heard Mum and Chris running up the stairs.

"What the hell is going on?" Mum asked. "We can hear you outside in the street!"

Chris took one look at the scene – I was on the floor, scrapping like a wild cat, Stephen, fists clenched, was leaning over me.

"That's enough, Stephen," Chris said. "I won't have this violent behaviour in my house."

I took the chance to get to my feet and run out onto the landing. Mum sighed and rolled her eyes. *Sibling rivalry.* But Stephen wasn't done yet, and with me out of the way, he turned his rage towards Mum and Chris.

"Don't tell me how to behave!" he bawled. "Don't tell me anything!"

"I think you should leave," I heard Chris say. "Now."

With Stephen thundering down the stairs, I dashed into

his bedroom, grabbed his clothes from his wardrobe, and chucked them out of the window, onto the garden below.

"Don't come back!" I yelled. "Ever!"

Mum came to stand at my shoulder.

"No need for that, you stupid cow!" Stephen shouted angrily.

Granted, it was a minor retribution, throwing the clothes. It was childish. Possibly it was mean. But the symbolism could not have been more powerful.

"There was every need," I said softly to myself, as I closed the window and watched him pick up his clothes. Moments later, he was gone.

Stephen returned to live with Dad and life continued, on the outside, more peacefully than before. But at my core, I was far from at peace. I coped in the only way I knew how, packaging the rapes away along with the rest of the abuse, squashing them down, and pretending, even to myself, that none of it had ever happened. And the more I ignored it all, the more I pushed it away, the easier it became. Or so I told myself. It was like throwing an ugly old ornament into the loft.

In years to come, hopefully I would forget about it completely.

Chapter Nineteen

WEEKS AFTER Stephen left, I got my O level results. Good grades, as predicted, in Art and Needlework, my favourite subjects.

"Can I go to college, Mum?" I asked excitedly. "If I do well at college, there's a polytechnic course in Art which I really fancy. Can I apply? Please?"

Mum shook her head in exasperation.

"You've got a perfectly good job at the pub," she replied. "You don't need to go to college. You should concentrate on earning a wage. Join the real world, Sarah."

I wanted to retort that I would have loved to join the real world, instead of the alternative hell where I was trapped. But I said nothing. It seemed my dream of studying art would remain just that.

The following month, Mum and Chris got married. I was chosen to be bridesmaid, and I sewed the dress myself; cream silk with chocolate lace overlaid, and matching ankle socks. Mum wore a lovely cream dress and she looked beautiful. Stephen came back for the big day, but we barely spoke to each other. I'd heard he had settled back with Dad, which left me feeling immeasurably sad. There was no hope for him now. Perhaps there never was.

"I can't stay long," he told my mother. "I'm travelling back to Somerset tonight."

I knew she was pleased he'd made the effort and not for the first time, I was torn right down the middle. Mum loved Stephen, he was her son, he was my brother. I felt like the fly in the ointment, like an annoying affliction. Why did I have to bring trouble wherever I went? Why couldn't I just block out the past, leave it where it was, and forget it had ever happened? The wedding, despite my misgivings, was lovely. Chris was a good man, and I was glad they'd made their relationship official.

"Congratulations," I smiled, and I meant it.

The atmosphere in the house, after their wedding, was light and joyful. Yet between Mum and I, there was still so much animosity, so much that went unspoken.

The antagonism festered like a wound, hidden under an inadequate sticking plaster, but always there. I wanted us to be close, I longed for that tie, just as much as when I was small. But the wall was there, and it felt like every time I knocked a brick out, she hastily put two back in.

Since leaving Dad she was undoubtedly more affectionate and more relaxed. However, I was learning that it was only superficial, at least where I was concerned. Scratch under the layers and she was as distant and faraway as ever. She never seemed to be genuine, she was never her real self. And even when we did talk, it felt to me that she was overly picky too;

constantly criticising and finding fault with everything I did. Perhaps I was oversensitive. I was admittedly lacking in confidence, and I took everything to heart. But Mum appeared to relish the opportunity to pull me to pieces. And then when I got upset, she'd jump in with her stock refrain:

"Don't be a cry-baby please."

She never seemed interested in why I was crying. She didn't want to hear my problems, she just wanted them to go away. I was upset by her dismissing my education, kicking my ambitions and my dreams to the kerb, as though they didn't matter. I had friends who were going off to college and, naturally, I wanted to join them. I had a real talent for Art, so many teachers had told me so. But Mum just wouldn't budge. She almost seemed to take a grim delight in holding me back, instead of helping me forwards. The deadline for the college course passed and, quietly, I mourned another missed opportunity. Then I spotted an advert for a Youth Training Scheme in jewellery making. This way, I'd earn a small wage, whilst training on the job, which I thought might appeal to Mum.

"What do you think?" I asked. "Can I do it? Please? I'd love to make jewellery and I think I'd be good at it. I'd earn a bit of money, and I could keep my job at the pub, part-time, to pay my way."

But Mum shook her head.

"You need to go full time at the pub," she retorted. "You don't know the meaning of hard work. You can't have everything in life handed to you."

I choked back the torrent of indignation that rose within

me. I'd had nothing handed to me except huge helpings of pain and sadness.

Nothing at all.

****

Despite my disappointment at missing out on college, working at the pub full time was fun. I had good friends, a busy social life, and I loved zipping around on my scooter. I heard nothing from Dad or Stephen and as each day passed, I interred the trauma deeper still.

Aged 17, I started dating a boy, Sam, who lived in a nearby town. My friends were all in relationships and I didn't want to be the odd one out. Sam was my first serious boyfriend, and at first, we seemed to get along fine. But as we became increasingly intimate, I felt myself retreating back into myself and away from him. Physically and emotionally, I couldn't bear to have anyone near me and yet at the same time, I craved affection and love.

I was eager to sleep with him, not because I wanted to have sex, but because I was desperate for it to be over. I just wanted to be like everyone else. I saw sex as a hurdle I had to overcome, another challenge. Realising I could not face it sober, I anaesthetised my anxiety with Babycham and white wine and then I told Sam I was ready. As far as he knew, and my friends knew, this was my first time ever having sex. I hoped I might believe it myself, eventually. And essentially, I now know that was true. The rapes by my father and my brother were not sex, they were violations, atrocities, outrages. And yet I feared they would darken and blight every relationship I had, for the rest of my life.

Sam and I were together for around a year, and though the physical side was excruciating for me, at other times we had fun together. But as the months passed, he began to remark on my agitation before we kissed or became intimate. He also noticed that I was blind drunk on almost every date night. One evening, he said to me:

"Why don't you like having sex with me?"

A cold sheen formed across my forehead. Caught off-guard, I didn't know how to respond. I owed him an almost-honest reply, especially since his own confidence had clearly been affected by my trauma. Perhaps too, my lips were loosened a little by the alcohol, because I mumbled:

"I was sexually abused when I was younger. I find it hard to get close to anyone, I'm sorry."

I didn't tell him who my abusers were, and he didn't ask. He just stared, open-mouthed. All my life, I had envisaged this, rehearsed it, planned it out. And when it came, as is often the way, it was something of a feeble anti-climax. Sam was the first person I'd confided in, and though I gave him no names and no details, the moment was seismic for me. But for Sam, it was pressure and responsibility he didn't need. The revelation was too much for him to cope with, he was just a teenager himself and was not equipped even to offer me the usual platitudes.

"Wow," he said eventually. "Wasn't expecting that."

It marked the end of our relationship and we finished officially soon afterwards. Mostly, I felt relief. I'd wanted a boyfriend so I could blend in with all my pals, and I could fit in with the crowd. But deep down I knew I could have all the accoutrements I liked, the boyfriend, the job, the scooter, the hairstyle. But all that was simply a veneer. At heart I was damaged, and I was broken, and I would never be a normal girl.

I was due to turn 18 in April 1987, and since my birthday would fall over Easter weekend, I began badgering Mum to let me have a party.

"It's bank holiday, so everyone will come," I wheedled. "Please, Mum. I can help with the arrangements."

I wanted to point out that Stephen had had a party; that Stephen always seemed to get his own way with everything. But I didn't. Eventually, she said:

"Go on then, just a small one."

At short notice it was difficult to find a venue, but eventually Nan announced the function room in their local pub was free.

"I've spoken to the landlady, she'll do a buffet and we can use their DJ," she said.

"Oh, maybe we should book that," Mum said.

"I already did," Nan winked. "Didn't want to miss out."

My heart filled with warmth. I knew I could count on Nan.

I had a perm done before my big day and bought myself a new white dress. My birthday cake was hexagonal, with pink and white cream icing. All my friends and family came to the party – and there was no sign of my father or of Stephen.

"Best birthday ever," I said to Mum. "Thank you."

Soon after, a cousin my age came to stay, and Mum told her

she could share my room, which had twin beds. She didn't check it with me, but I was used to that, and I was quite looking forward to the company. But, as the days passed, I became more and more disgruntled. My cousin, unlike me, was untidy and her stuff was all over the place, her clothes on the floor, her dirty tissues on the chest of drawers, her half-filled mugs of tea on the bedside table.

"Can you at least keep your mess on your side of the room?" I asked, scooping up an armful of her discarded belongings and plonking them onto her single bed.

She just raised an eyebrow, as though I was the one being unreasonable. We were not getting on well at all and sharing a room was becoming increasingly awkward. She seemed to get special treatment off Mum, too. After work, she was allowed to eat her meals on a tray in front of the TV, whereas I had to eat at the dining table. Now working full time, I was paying my mother a weekly 'keep' to help cover my bills. So when I found out my untidy cousin was paying nothing at all, I felt even more aggrieved. It felt like the same old story, all over again. My mother just wouldn't support me or take my side. Metaphorically, she had dumped me in the corner, to wait for a beating from my father. Spilling over with teenage defiance and swirling hormones, I decided to confront her.

"Why am I paying keep and not her?" I asked. "It's not fair."

Depending on my hours I paid Mum as much as £30 a week, not a small sum in those days. But for me, the money was not the real issue.

"It's nothing to do with you," my mother snapped.

"It's everything to do with me and it's not fair," I repeated. "She trashes my room, she eats her meals on a tray, and she doesn't pay a penny towards her bills. I don't understand why you're so mean to me."

My voice cracked and wavered and my eyes filled with tears.

"Oh, Sarah, don't start crying again," Mum said impatiently. "Such a cry-baby."

She could not resist adding in that little jibe, and it was like slipping a splinter under my fingernail. For some reason, it was the final straw. That small phrase was enough to unleash years of resentment and deep-seated injustice.

"Why do you never support me?" I asked, the tears pouring now down my cheeks. "You never favour me, and you find fault with every single thing I do. All my life, you've left me to it. Why could you not just take my side, for once? For once, Mum?"

Mum stared at me in astonishment; more, I think, at my audacity than at the content of my argument. And there was more, rising up my throat like bile, a tide I could not suppress.

Why did you let Dad beat me? Why did you never ask what was wrong with me? Why did you not notice when I was being sexually abused and raped right under your nose? Why did you not protect me? Why, why why?

But I swallowed it all back down again.

Even with my new-found courage, I could not have shared this with my mother and my pleas remained suspended at the threshold between thought and speech. Already, by complaining about my cousin, by challenging my mother as a parent, I felt I had said too much. Even though I had not mentioned Dad, the ghosts of the past hovered over us both. These days, Mum never mentioned him at all. She had closed the door on her marriage, and on everything it stood for, and it was firmly locked and bolted. There was an unspoken rule in the house that we did not talk about Dad. Mum wanted to forget about that awful chapter, and I was expected to do that too. It was as though she had wiped the past two decades from her memory and, in exchange for her raising me and showing me occasional kindness, I had to do the same. In many ways, that deadly thread of secrecy and lies had travelled with us, from Somerset to Wales.

"You should be more grateful," Mum said, as I mopped my eyes with a tissue. "You have a home, you have food on the table, and a warm bed. I don't know what's the matter with you half of the time."

Miserably, I nodded. I agreed with one thing, at least. I didn't know what the matter with me was either.

After our fall-out, I was resigned to looking for a place of my own. If Mum and I were ever going to get along, we needed some space. I soon found a nice, neat little first floor bedsit, on a high street behind Woolworths, around 20 minutes away from Nan's house and 15 minutes from home. The rent was £26 a week plus bills. It was just a square room with a single bed, wardrobe and chest of drawers, and a shared kitchen and bathroom. But it spelled freedom for me. It was perfect. I sold my beloved scooter to raise the deposit and used all my savings too.

The Letter

"I'll take it," I beamed, handing over my first month's rent.

Moving in, I made it my own with posters and little personal touches. Mum visited, and though we were friends again, she did not offer to help me in any way. I was on my own; financially and, more so, emotionally. Our relationship was back on its default setting, cool, but not cold. Nan came to see my new place too, loaded up with biscuits and cake and a set of towels as a house-warming gift.

"I'm very proud of you," she smiled. "It's a nice little flat."

I got a new job in a factory, making school trousers for the big stores like BHS. I was paid by piecework, so the more I sewed, the more I earned, and that suited me just fine. Ironically, I was now putting my creative skills to good use after all. I settled in immediately and loved it at the factory, the staff were all friendly and the atmosphere was fun. We worked hard, Monday to Thursday, 7am – 5.30pm. On Fridays, we finished at 1pm, when, clutching our brown paper pay packets, we went straight to the pub to spend our hard-earned cash. I loved being part of the team. I enjoyed that feeling of belonging, just as when I'd lived with Nan.

Despite my Friday nights out, I learned to budget sensibly, collecting 50ps for the electric meter and setting aside money for my weekly food shop. I saved hard too and booked my first overseas holiday with a pal from work, a cheap package deal to the Costa Brava. We spent the week dancing on tables and sleeping off hangovers. We barely even saw the sun.

"I've had the best time of my life," I grinned, as we boarded the plane home.

My childhood memories were like a stone in my shoe, an

uncomfortable reminder which, if pushed to the edge, could almost be forgotten. Almost.

My mind bounced from hope to despair and back again with alarming regularity. Sometimes, I'd run a wobbly seam through on the sewing machine at work and have to throw the ruined garment in the bin. We usually had a big pile of rejects by the end of the week. And, as I peered into the bin, the trousers took on an almost human-like melancholy, lying there helplessly, destined for landfill. Like myself, they were soiled, worthless, ruined and awaiting a fate they could not control.

"I will shoot you, I will shoot you all."

Chapter Twenty

NOW I was living on my own, I saw much more of Nan and Grandad. I'd ride down the coast at weekends, and Nan always had a welcome and a hot dinner waiting. If I visited on a Saturday, before a night out, she'd insist on cooking up a real feast.

"You need to line your belly before you hit the town with your pals," she said. "You must never drink on an empty stomach."

After we'd eaten, I would shower and change at her house, blow-drying my hair and doing my make-up, before meeting my friends. Nan closely monitored my styles and my outfits. She loved to give her opinion.

"You can't go out without a coat," she'd say, shaking her head. "Not in this weather. You'll catch your death. Put a pair of tights on at least, love. Take a hat and a pair of gloves."

I rolled my eyes, but I secretly loved her fussing. She was like a mother hen, clucking and clicking her beak, keeping her young ones safe under her feathers. One week, with a full pay-packet in my pocket, I announced I was taking her and Grandad out to a restaurant. They rarely treated themselves.

"I want to give you a break from cooking," I told Nan. "Let me look after you, for a change."

We had a lovely meal and afterwards, I suggested a nightcap for Nan to round the evening off.

"What about a whisky?" I said.

"Oh, I don't know," she shrieked, pulling a funny face as though I'd suggested she should drink the whole bottle. "I'm not a big drinker, you know that."

"Go on," I wheedled.

After a few moments of consideration, she winked and conceded: "Oh ok, just a small one."

I ordered her a double at the bar, and pints of bitter and lager for Grandad and me. Nan gulped at the size of the drink but polished it off anyway.

"Can I ask a question?" I said, as I sipped my lager, and they both nodded. "When you've been married for so long, like you two, do you stay together out of love, or just out of habit?"

They replied in unison.

"It's love," Grandad said sincerely.

"It's habit," Nan quipped.

We laughed so much, I spat a mouthful of my drink all over my dress. And I knew then, no matter what trauma and pain had been dumped upon me, I would always be blessed to have Nan and Grandad by my side.

Late in the summer of 1988, I was working in the bar, washing glasses, when I sensed someone was looking at me.

The Letter

"Can I buy you a drink after work?" a voice asked, and as I stood up straight, I saw a good-looking bloke smiling at me.

I hesitated. Even from that first brief encounter, I could see he was not only gorgeous, but that he knew it too. He radiated confidence, in the same way I probably exuded a lack of it.

"Go on," said my pal, who was working the same shift. "What have you got to lose?"

I'd been single for a while, and so, returning his smile, I nodded. He waited until my shift was finished and then took me to another bar nearby. His name was Harry and, as we talked, I felt myself warming to him. He was funny and chatty, yet he was a good listener too. Generous and attentive, he bought all my drinks. But the resistance was still there, deep inside me, like a thick carapace around my heart.

"I'm not really looking for anything serious," I told him.

"Me neither," Harry replied. "I'm joining the forces, so I'll be going away soon."

It was a perfect arrangement which suited us both. As our relationship developed, I relied on alcohol, again, to dampen down my misgivings and carry me through the physical side of things. Just as when I was small, I learned to divide parts of myself into chunks. I managed to neatly separate the physical and emotional aspects of dating, and inwardly, I remained quite distant.

Harry was posted away on training with his regiment, and he sent me long love letters. Even so, reading his compliments and his promises, I didn't quite believe it. I just didn't think I deserved to be treasured like this. Many times, I started a letter to send back to him, but it felt forced and false. I wanted to fall in love, I really did. But I just didn't know how.

'Dear Harry, I can't live without you.'

No, that was too dramatic.

'Dear Harry, I miss your smile.'

Too soppy.

'Dear Harry, I have a huge secret hiding inside me, and I need help.'

Too dangerous.

The following February, I missed a period and was dumbfounded when a pregnancy test came back positive. I was on the contraceptive pill and had naively believed it was foolproof. I hadn't even considered that I might fall pregnant. Aged 19, I was a curious cocktail of childish innocence and world-weariness. Whilst I'd endured unspeakable horrors within my own four walls, I was, at the same time, very unsure of how to behave outside of them. Certainly, I struggled with relationships. I had no idea what was expected of me and what I should expect from others. My role models, my father and my older brother, had poisoned my mind with a skewed and negative perspective of men and I just didn't know what was normal.

At first, with the pregnancy test in my trembling hand, I felt out of my depth. I wasn't sure I should even keep the baby. I was only just about managing to look after myself in my little bedsit. But when I finally plucked up courage to confide in Harry, he was over the moon.

"It's brilliant news!" he beamed. "I'll help you, don't worry. We'll be together forever."

The Letter

I told Mum too, bracing myself for a barrage of criticism. But to my surprise she was thrilled by the news that I was about to make her a grandmother.

"I'll help as much as I can," she promised. "I know you're young, but you're not on your own."

Again, she had wrong-footed me. Just as I had feared our bond was stretched to breaking point, she reined me back in with her love, and gave me the confidence to continue. In those first few months, my pregnancy went well and, as a new life grew inside me, my love for Harry blossomed too. Finally, I began to believe it might happen for me after all, a baby, a life partner, a family of my own. Now, suddenly, my love letters flowed easily.

'I love you so much, Harry.' I wrote. 'I can't wait for our baby to arrive.'

But as the weeks wore on, I became anaemic. I was constantly exhausted, often in and out of hospital. I went on maternity leave from the trouser factory, but could barely find enough money to pay my rent, let alone save for my new arrival. Harry was away most of the time with his job and I felt isolated and out of my depth. Now, to add to my other worries, I was struggling financially, too.

"Why don't you move back home?" Mum suggested. "Just until the baby is born. I can look after you both."

Her generosity came so completely out of the blue that it moved me to tears.

"If you don't mind, I'd love that," I said.

She kept her word, keeping an eye on me, reassuring me that swollen ankles, stretchmarks and twinges were all part of the process. Just to have someone around who had done it all before was a comfort. And she helped out financially too. One afternoon, she took me out shopping and bought a new pram.

"Thank you," I said. "I don't know what I'd do without you."

My pregnancy had the added bonus of bringing Mum and I together, and I treasured our new closeness. When Harry next came home, he took my hand in his and said:

"Sarah, will you marry me? I want us to be a proper family, for our baby."

I was simultaneously overjoyed and devastated. I loved Harry. But in that moment, I felt like a fraud. I realised I couldn't take such a big step, couldn't make him my husband, without first letting him know who I really was.

"What's wrong?" he asked. "Why the tears?"

To my alarm, the tears flowed even faster. And in a rush, like a dam bursting, it all tumbled out.

"You have a right to know who you're marrying," I sobbed. "I was abused, as a little girl, by my dad and later my older brother."

Harry's jaw dropped. He didn't know what to say. He had met Dad once, briefly, but didn't know him well.

"Shouldn't you go to the police?" he stuttered eventually. "They can't get away with it. They should be in prison."

"No!"

I shook my head firmly, trying to dislodge the image of those guns.

"No. I can't report it. I just want to put it all behind me. I thought you should know, that's all. I understand if you don't want to get married now."

Harry seemed bewildered.

"It makes no difference, I love you," he insisted.

But at that moment, if only in my mind, a fissure opened up between us. It was no more than a sliver, a slight crack. But with each day, it inched wider. And wider still. I was losing him, and I knew it. At my next ante-natal check, the midwife measured my stomach and said the baby wasn't growing as expected.

"You're very thin," she remarked. "You need to eat more."

I did my best, but I had always been naturally slim and slight, and now, I just didn't have the appetite. And so, for the remaining nine weeks of pregnancy, I was admitted into hospital. I managed to get a message to Harry, and he came home again as soon as he could. I couldn't wait to see him. But when I spotted his face, at the entrance to the ward, his smile was tight.

"Look, I can't cope with the distance any longer," he said as he reached my bedside. "I'm sorry, I think it's better if we end things now."

I was shattered. I thought back to that slight fissure, now a gaping chasm. My secret had driven us apart. Along with all my other problems, I was facing the prospect of raising a child on my own.

"You need to forget all about him," Mum said, typically business-like. "No point crying, Sarah. I'll help. You have lots of support from me, and Nan too."

She was not a shoulder to cry on. She never would be. But

she was materialising, day by day, into the sort of mother I would have loved, as a child. There remained that implied understanding between us, that we would not discuss my father, or anything that had taken place during my childhood. We pretended he had never existed, focussing only on the future, on the new baby. And that suited me perfectly. I had no desire to dredge up old ghosts when I had another life to consider.

Mum was my birthing partner when I went into labour, two weeks early, in August 1989. As I breathed through the contractions, the midwife ran through a standard set of questions and asked:

"Have you ever had a blood transfusion?"

"No," I panted, but to my surprise, Mum interrupted and said:

"Actually, yes, you have. When you were small."

I'd had no idea. I thought perhaps she was referring to the time I had fallen from my bike, or the climbing frame. Or it might have been one of the many falls from Fire. I didn't remember a transfusion, I didn't even remember any serious injuries, but I had more important issues to consider at the time.

My beautiful daughter, Lolly, was born soon after, weighing 6lbs 15ozs. She had jet black hair curling down to her neck and the nurses and midwives came from other wards to admire her.

"Where's that baby with the mop of hair?" they all asked.

As I held my daughter in my arms, I felt, without doubt, the weight of responsibility, but with it a fierce wave of maternal love. I knew then, I would manage, no matter what. Mum was besotted with her new granddaughter and stayed at the hospital until way past visiting hours. Though she didn't say it, she seemed intent on making up for past mistakes, if not with me, then with her grandchild.

A couple of days later, Lolly and I were due to be discharged and were waiting for Mum to come and pick us up. I was in a side room on my own when, without warning, the door opened and Dad marched in.

"So," he said, gazing at the cot. "This is my granddaughter then?"

For a few moments, I was mute with shock. I'd had no contact with him for years. I hadn't even told him I was pregnant. How on earth did he know? Lying in bed, in my nightie, I felt alarmingly vulnerable and exposed, my eyes flicking to the door, wishing a staff nurse would walk past. And yet, what would I have done? I didn't want to reveal the abuse. I didn't want to cause a fuss. I wanted to be a mummy, I wanted a happy family, I wanted a perfect future for my child. Again, I was split down the middle. Two Sarahs. Two lives.

"She is very cute," Dad said, though he made no effort to approach her, or me, which I was thankful for.

He hadn't brought a present, or even a card. He didn't even have anything more to say. In the silence, my mind was whirring at top speed. I felt like a car with brake failure. I heard his belt clinking. I saw those blue bedroom walls. I smelled the stale cigars. I had thousands of questions, recriminations, accusations, rushing wildly around my brain. And yet, I could not think of a single thing to say. In the event, I remained quiet, my default setting. Dad only stayed a matter of minutes and then he was gone. Immediately, I got out of bed to check on Lolly, even though he hadn't been near her. Afterwards, shakily, I relayed the incident to Mum.

"Who on earth told him you'd had a baby?" She asked.

"No idea," I replied, shaking my head.

It was only later, after I was home, that I learned an aunt had informed him, without telling me.

"He has a right to know he has a grandchild," she told me piously.

He has no rights! I wanted to scream. *None.*

But I nodded, obediently. After years of practice, I was an expert at keeping quiet.

Chapter Twenty-One

BACK AT Mum's, she was a doting grandmother to Lolly.

"You get some sleep," she insisted. "I'll get up with her tonight. You know, I quite like doing the night-time feeds."

We never discussed it, as was our way, but again it was her way of atoning. Lolly brought us all together — Nan, Mum and me, four generations of females.

"She looks just like you," I told Mum. "I can really see the resemblance, especially when she smiles."

Mum glowed with pride. She and Lolly had such a lovely connection. Lolly would giggle and coo every time she heard Mum's voice. I watched them both closely and quite unexpectedly, through Mum's example, I learned how to be a parent myself. My own childhood had taught me how not to raise a child, but now Mum was a grandmother, she was so much more attentive.

I'd been on a waiting list for my own place since Harry and I had split, but when a council flat became available in Aberystwyth, I had mixed feelings. Mum and Chris were living in Pembrokeshire now, so I was keen to move back to the area I knew, near to Nan and many of my friends. But – and I could not quite believe it – it hit me just how much I would miss my mother. We had come full circle. From being peripheral and withdrawn she was now at the very nucleus of my world.

"Oh, I'll miss you both," she said, as we packed her car up ready to leave. "But I'm always here if you need me."

My little council flat was bleak and bare, and those first few weeks on my own were lonely. I was 20 years old, a single mum, with not much money and a fractured family network. But my biggest obstacle was my lack of confidence in my own ability to raise a child. I spent night after night, sitting in on my own and, through the silence, the memories slithered back in, like worms coming up through the soil. Everywhere, there were sharp little reminders, scattered like needles, of what it was to be a parent and so, by definition, of how tragically my father had failed me.

The memories swarmed around me like wasps and fiercely, I batted them away. I could not afford to think of this, not now. To be a good mother myself, my own horror had to be packaged away. It was one or the other, that was how I saw it. I had to completely forget my own past in order to focus purely on my daughter's future. I owed it to her to keep quiet and to keep her safe from my father's threats. And so, just like Mum, I denied my own trauma, now more than ever before. I locked it away, conscious I was doing the same as her. Again, the irony was not lost on me. But through the prism of motherhood, I understood her motivations and I had empathy with her coping mechanisms. I used them myself, too.

The Letter

As Lolly and I settled into our new life, I set about trying to find work. I got a job as a carer, but the shift pattern didn't fit in with looking after Lolly at all. I had moved an hour and a half's journey away from Mum, and so she was unable to help with childcare. Nan was nearer but was still a bus ride away. With no support close by, I had to give up my job and concentrate on being a full-time mum. As time went on, I settled into the role and mostly, I managed well on my own. But when Lolly was learning to walk, I needed surgery on a weak ankle, which left me hobbling around on crutches for weeks.

"Let me take Lolly," Mum insisted. "I'll have her at my house, just until you're back on your feet."

"Are you sure?" I asked.

I didn't fancy us being apart, but I had been worried about caring for a toddler on my own when I couldn't even walk myself.

"Of course," Mum replied. "I've missed her so much, I'd love to have her to stay. It's a good excuse to spoil her."

It was comforting to know I had someone I could rely on, if not for me, then for my daughter. The months passed, and I remained close to Mum and Chris and, as always, Nan and Grandad too. There was no word from Dad, and I didn't allow myself to think past the relief of his absence. But after Lolly turned two, I answered a knock at the door to find Stephen and a male friend outside.

"Surprise!" Stephen smiled, stepping inside. "I got your address off the family and thought we'd call in."

I was stunned. As I scrambled my thoughts, I felt typically

divided. I wanted him out of there, I wanted to slam the door, I wanted to scream at the top of my voice for him never to return.

He's a rapist! the other Sarah shouted. *You should call the police! Now!*

But also, I wanted a brother. An uncle for Lolly. A family. Normality.

Perhaps it was a mistake, I told myself. *It was a long time. He's changed. He's grown up. Maybe he's sorry, even.*

The other Sarah continued to protest in the background, but I ignored her. I flicked the kettle on and emptied a packet of digestives onto a plate.

"Help yourselves," I smiled, aware on one level how incongruous my behaviour was, whilst at the same time thrilled to see my brother again. Even so, I did not leave him alone with Lolly even for an instant. When I needed the loo, I made an excuse and took Lolly with me. I was in denial, yes. But it only went so far.

"We should stay in touch," Stephen said, as he drained his cup. "Been nice seeing you."

"Let's do that," I nodded, knowing it wouldn't happen. But around a year later, I got a wedding invitation through the post. Stephen was getting married. Again, I was mired in muddy confusion. Should I speak out? Ruin the big day? Break the bride's heart? My predicament became yet more weighty when Mum called me, bubbling over with excitement.

"I'm getting a new outfit," she told me. "I can't wait to get the family together. I'll babysit Lolly at the wedding if you like, then you can have a dance and a few drinks."

The Letter

I didn't know what to say. How could I go along with this façade, watching my brother get married, after he had raped me. Yet what was the alternative? I felt like a curse, a jinx, a harbinger of bad news. With one sentence, I could destroy my entire family, set it alight and watch it burn. The responsibility of this was almost as terrifying as the abuse itself. And Stephen's threat was never far from my mind:

"If you tell anyone, I'll say you wanted it."

Even aged 23, I could not take the risk he might follow it through. I could not bear the shame. Not once did it occur to me, even as a mother myself, that no reasonable person would believe him for a moment. I was a child. He was an adult. It was clearly and obviously rape. But still I blamed myself. I hadn't yet replied to the wedding invitation when Stephen called me.

"Would you like to be a bridesmaid?" He asked.

Again, I was blindsided. I had so much to say, but the words dried in my throat. What was this? Some sort of sick apology? Or a warped bribe, a ham-fisted attempt to keep me quiet?

"No," I stuttered eventually. "No, thank you."

A few weeks later, I attended a joint hen and stag night and found I got on really well with Stephen's fiancé, Dara.

"I really wish you'd be a bridesmaid," she said. "If not you, what about Lolly? Will you let her be my bridesmaid instead?"

I couldn't think how to say no. Besides, I knew Lolly, now four years old, would enjoy being the centre of attention and dressing up in fancy clothes. I couldn't bring myself to shatter Dara's illusions of Stephen, but I was nonetheless saddled with a debilitating guilt for keeping quiet.

You're letting her marry a rapist. You should have told her.

"If you tell anyone, I'll say you wanted it."

"If you open your mouth, I will shoot you all."

It was exhausting. I could see no end to the cycle of conflicting voices which looped through my mind.

"Thank you," I smiled eventually. "I'm sure Lolly will love that."

Later in the evening, I got chatting to another guest, Andy, who was a friend of Stephen's. To my surprise, we really hit it off, he made me laugh and paid me lots of compliments. And talking to him was a much-needed distraction from the arguments between one side of my conscience and the other.

"I've really enjoyed spending time with you," he said. "I'm hoping you feel the same way."

I smiled. There hadn't really been anyone serious since Harry. I'd had some brief encounters on nights out, confused and awkward liaisons, always when Lolly was staying over with Mum. Those one-night stands were an attempt to boost my confidence and well-being, but perversely and unsurprisingly they did just the opposite. I slept with strangers to feel loved. I ended up feeling despised. I'd drink myself into a stupor on those nights, I'd added vodka into my Babycham by now, and quite often, I passed out before I even got home. Once, I awoke laid out full-length in my doorway, with my neighbour staring at me over the fence in bemusement.

"Good night?" she asked, and I grinned sheepishly.

Again, I was using alcohol as an avoidance technique, a

crutch and an anaesthetic. Wrapping myself in a blanket of booze somehow deadened the hurt and the shame, for a short while at least. But because I didn't drink regularly, I didn't for a moment recognise I might have a drink problem. Like all my other issues, it was pushed aside, buried, and ultimately denied. So, when Andy took a shine to me, at the stag and hen do, it was a nice change to be flattered and fussed over. It felt like I was borrowing scenes from someone else's life.

"Could I see you again?" he asked. "Would you let me take you to dinner?"

"Yes," I smiled. "That sounds lovely."

We started dating and later I introduced him to Lolly. He made such an effort with her, and that made me love him all the more. We attended Stephen's wedding together, all smiles. But when I spotted Dad among the guests, I felt the blood draining from my face.

Both of my rapists, here, in one room. One is getting married. The other is the father of the groom.

It was like a plot from a horribly far-fetched film. On the outside, I stayed as calm and composed as possible, though I could not stop a tremor in my hand. Through the service, I gnawed at my fingernails, right down to the skin. At the reception, Dad made a beeline for Andy and me.

"Why haven't you been in touch?" he asked me. "I haven't seen you for ages. Or my granddaughter for that matter."

Disconcerted, I hesitated. Even though he was making demands, this wasn't his usual tone. He was more light-hearted and friendly. Jolly even. He was playing a role again, being the charming builder, probably more for Andy's benefit than mine.

"You haven't been in touch either," I reminded him warily.

To my astonishment, he nodded in agreement.

"That's true," he said. "But I would like to be. I want to know how you are. I'm glad we can air these issues, Sarah."

Stumped, I simply bowed my head. The issue we could never raise, of course, lay prone between us, like a great slimy slug. A part of me could not believe his audacity. Yet absurdly, I really wanted to believe him, too. I was desperate for everything to be alright. I looked around me at the perfect family scene, my daughter, impossibly cute in her bridesmaid dress; my brother, the smiling groom; my father, jovial and proud in his smart suit. My role, I understood, was to act out the part of mother, daughter and sister. I was not the protagonist in my own story. I was simply a character in my father's drama. I was imprisoned and defined by the abuse, and I always would be. It was best for everyone if my secret stayed where it belonged, obscured from view. Perhaps, I persuaded myself, it had never happened. Maybe it was a far-fetched film script after all.

Best just to let sleeping rapists lie.

Chapter Twenty-Two

ANDY AND I had been together six months when we went on a night out, around the pubs, before ending up in a nightclub. I was dancing to Madness, oblivious to all else, when I suddenly spotted Andy up on the stage, holding the DJ's microphone.

"Sarah," he called, searching for my face in the crowd. "Will you marry me?"

A huge cheer erupted, and all eyes were on me. Blinking as the lights went up, I tried to hide my surprise. Flattered and alarmed in equal measure, I had to think fast.

"Yes!" I stuttered, because it felt like the only acceptable response. "Yes, of course!"

It wasn't that I didn't love Andy, more that I was unsure of myself. At my core, I didn't feel worthy of marriage. I wanted to tell him about the abuse, explain how I was a bad bet, how he should run for the hills and leave me behind. But I remembered the breakdown of my relationship with Harry, and I was frightened that if I confided in Andy, it would happen again. I was also conscious of Andy's close friendship with Stephen. I could not predict how Andy would react to my secret. What if he confronted Stephen, worse still, my Dad? I decided I couldn't take that risk. Staying silent felt like a betrayal. But speaking out would be a death wish. I was caught in an impossible situation. That summer, as we were planning for our big day, I found out I was pregnant.

"Sooner than expected, but it's great news," Andy smiled.

We brought our wedding forward, and I had my dress altered slightly, to allow for my bump. As we were finalising our plans, I got a call from my father.

"Just checking when and where I need to be for the big day," he said. "I'll be giving you away."

It was a statement, not a question. There was so much entitlement and arrogance in his voice, it made me want to weep. How could he really expect to be invited, less still give me away? He had battered me, humiliated me and raped me and now he wanted to play the proud father at my wedding. It was beyond grotesque. I thought back to Stephen's bridesmaid request — was this a similar ploy? Was he covering his tracks, trying to prove what a wonderful father he was? *Well, he walked her down the aisle, so he can't be that much of a monster...*

But the truth was, even if Dad hadn't presumed to give me away, I would have asked him to anyway. Looking back now, I cannot fathom my own thought processes. I do not understand my behaviour. I was so compliant, so under his control, that I did as I was told, regardless of how twisted it seemed. I remembered his guns. I remembered his threats. I thought of my daughter's cherubic little face, and I felt I had no option.

"Yes," I replied. "Course, I'd love you to give me away."

The Letter

Even as an adult, I was split down the middle; two people, completely diverse. One Sarah wanted a traditional father, a white wedding, a normal life. The other Sarah had been abused and she remained at home, trapped by her own trauma. She was not invited to the wedding.

Before our big day, Lolly and I moved to Somerset, to live with Andy, a decision which was riddled with triggers for me, but again, I said nothing. It was like an amateur form of self-hypnosis, if I told myself often enough that the abuse didn't happen, then I would eventually believe it. Mum didn't approve of the move, possibly she resented the links with our past. But she was also worried about losing touch with Lolly.

"That will never happen," I promised. "I know how much you love her."

We had a register office wedding, in October 1993, and Dad turned up with a new partner. As he walked me down the aisle, I blinked away flash reminders of our shared past, the blue bedroom walls, the brown leather belt, the scratchy beard, the gun draped oh so casually across his desk. It had all happened to another little girl, I told myself firmly. Not to me. I had become so expert at disassociation, I actually half-believed my own lies. I searched for Nan's face in the congregation, trying to tap into her scent and her warmth. But as I said my vows, the other Sarah hovered above me, gatecrashing my big day, her face screwed up and crimson with anger.

Tell them! she yelled. *Tell them all what he did to you! And Stephen too! They should be behind bars, not sitting in a pew with fancy suits on! Tell them!*

But I could not do it, and she knew that, and it made her angrier still. After the ceremony, Mum pulled me aside.

"Why did he give you away? Why did you let that happen?" She hissed.

I had no answer. Or at least, not one she would want to hear. Equally, I could have asked her why she was so opposed to my father giving me away. Yet I suspected she'd have no answer either.

* * * *

I had always been slim and slight. I was 5'2" and, pre-pregnancy, weighed a little under eight stone. But as my bump grew, my relationship with food became increasingly fraught. I began skipping meals, without consciously admitting why. I'd cook every day for Andy and Lolly, but snack on cheese and crackers myself. Maybe I'd nibble on a slice of toast. Sometimes, I'd eat nothing at all.

"Are you ill?" Andy frowned. "Why aren't you sitting down with us for dinner? You need to eat, Sarah. Think of the baby."

The midwife endorsed his concerns.

"The baby is smaller than we'd like," she said. "We'll need to admit you into hospital if you don't start gaining weight. Why aren't you eating? Do you feel nauseous? Is that the problem?"

I shook my head numbly.

"I don't know what the problem is," I lied.

How to tell her that in the very darkest recesses of my

mind, lurking amongst the cobwebs, the spirits and the spiders, there was a glacial hand which brushed my face when I slept. And with the hand, was a disembodied voice, cackling, crowing, hissing.

You let it happen. You let him do it.

Stopping eating was not a physical issue. It was a punishment. A judgement. A life sentence. I had let myself be raped. I had let myself be abused. And so, I did not deserve to eat. Worried by the midwife's warning, I managed to force-feed myself just enough to keep my baby healthy, whilst I muddled along. I was exhausted and wearied by the lack of calories. But I thrived on the control. I relished the penance. In my dreams, I welcomed the cold hand on my face and the judgemental voice. I deserved it.

One afternoon, Andy and I were invited to a barbeque at the house where my father lived with his new partner. I accepted, determined to follow through with the pretence, confident I could carry it off. But as we parked, I was seized with a jangling fear, every nerve ending on high alert, as though my body was warning me against going inside. This was a step too far. Every house my father had owned had heaped horror and misery upon me. I could not allow it to happen again in a new place.

"I don't feel too well," I told Andy, cradling my baby bump in explanation. "I'll wait in the car until you're ready to leave."

"You sure?" he asked. "I'll just go inside and explain. I won't be long."

****

Our daughter, Donna, was born in March 1994, and though she was as fair as her sister was dark, they looked similar in other ways; the cute turned up little noses, the adorable rosebud mouths. This time around, as we left the hospital, I felt more self-assured, superficially at least. I was a couple of weeks from my 25th birthday, I had a husband and a home. Andy and I had moved from his rented flat into a three-storey converted farmhouse, ideal for raising a family. We were comfortably off too. Andy worked shifts in technology, and I had a part-time job as a carer. My in-laws lived nearby, and they were a great help with childcare. And at every holiday, and every Christmas, we travelled to South Wales to stay with Mum or Nan. Despite the distance, Mum continued to be a wonderful grandmother to my two girls. Cosmetically, we were settled and happy and quite typical. But my eating disorder simmered in the background, like a pot on the stove. And my greatest fears prowled alongside it. Andy and I had been married about 18 months when, out of the blue, I got a call from Stephen.

"Dad has been accused of sexually abusing a child," he said. "Have you heard anything about it?"

The words smacked into me like a sledgehammer. Breathing heavily, I clutched at the wall, the room spinning around me. Stephen, in the background, seemed to be speaking on fast forward. I couldn't make any sense of the words.

"I have to go," I whispered, and I hung up.

The silence slowly settled like dust around me, but my

heart pounded in my ears, so loud it was a physical assault. I was dazed and shaky, as though I had been hit over the head with a cricket bat. Yet I knew, with absolute clarity, what I had to do. Andy was at work, and I was home with the girls on my own. I took a few moments to steady myself and then I got busy. Frantically, haphazardly, I began throwing toys into bags. I dragged our holiday suitcases down from the loft and filled them with clothes.

"We're going away," I told the children brightly. "Off to the seaside! Off to see Nan!"

As I packed, I was reminded of my teenage self, whizzing around our house in Meare, throwing clothes into bin bags as we fled from my father. Over a decade later, I was doing it again. Any half-baked notions I'd had of happiness and normality were, I realised, no more than a cruel illusion. I scribbled a quick note for Andy, telling him we'd gone to Wales.

"Please don't worry," I wrote. "I have some stuff to sort out."

What else could I say?

My past is catching up with me and I have to run. I'm terrified of my father. Terrified he will shoot me. Terrified my daughters are in danger.

I drove through the night to Wales, staying a few nights with a friend before arranging to rent a flat in Aberystwyth from her. My pal, I think, assumed I'd been arguing with Andy, and she didn't ask too many questions. The whole time, I was so agitated and afraid that I couldn't think straight. I had no idea who had made the report about my father, but I felt certain a police investigation would eventually snake its way around to me. The game was up. Would he shoot me, actually shoot me? I wondered. Would he shoot my daughters too? To an outsider, it might sound fantastical and far-fetched. But I had seen the guns. I had witnessed the anger. I had felt the pain. I knew the threat was real. Andy followed us down to Wales, completely perplexed by my late-night disappearance.

"What's going on?" he demanded.

I understood his anger, but for his sake, I could not confide in him.

"It's me, not you," I said vaguely. "I have some family issues. You're better off without me, Andy."

When he realised that I wasn't prepared to return to Somerset, he offered to move to Wales, to give our marriage a chance. We both found work easily, and the girls settled in well. But I was in a permanent state of alarm, always waiting for news of my father. I was afraid to answer the door or the phone, in case it was the police, or worse, my father. It felt inevitable. I had never broken the law in my life, yet I felt like I had done something very wrong. I was running from my father, running from myself, running from the truth. But I knew I couldn't run forever. And I understood, of course, that being in Wales didn't offer any kind of immunity from danger. My father could track me down here, easily enough. The move from Somerset was irrational and illogical and it solved nothing. But I hadn't moved because I thought it was a good idea. I had moved because I had no other choice. Physically, I felt compelled to up and go.

Weeks passed and there was nothing from the police, nothing from my father, nothing from Stephen. But the lack of contact simply added to my feelings of doom.

"Why can't we go back to Somerset?" Andy asked.

I raised my shoulders in an exaggerated shrug, casting off all my trauma, just as I had when I was small.

"I can't say," I said. "I'm sorry."

I couldn't confide in Andy. Saying it out loud, even admitting it to myself, felt like a huge risk. In some absurd way, I hoped by burying it, deeper and deeper, I might actually extinguish it completely. With so much unsaid between us, Andy and I grew apart quickly and our marriage was over within the year.

In despair, I saw it as yet more confirmation that I was a failure. And in the foreground, dominating all my thoughts, all my time, was the spectre of the abuse. I could not even grieve the end of my marriage in peace, because I was haunted by ghoulish reminders of my father and my older brother.

Mine was an existence built on toxic landfill and I always felt it was a matter of time before they bulldozed back into my life and smashed it to bits once again. Sometimes, in the dead of night, I'd wake, drenched in sweat, my skin prickling with foreboding.

"I will shoot you. I will shoot you all."

Half paralysed by panic, I'd rush to check on my girls, bracing myself for a bloodbath, and instead finding them sleeping peacefully.

He doesn't even know where we live, I reminded myself. *He couldn't just turn up in the night and shoot us all. I've kept my secret; I've done as he said. He won't hurt us.*

But no matter what I told myself, I never felt truly safe. The walls of our home seemed paper thin, as if they could be ripped apart, screwed up and thrown away. With the big bad wolf at the door, we stood no chance of survival.

Little pigs, little pigs, let me come in.

Chapter Twenty-Three

JUST AS I was adjusting once more to life as a single mum, my friend served notice on my tenancy. Though I scoured the rentals in the local paper, I couldn't find anywhere else affordable.

Moving day came and the girls and I found ourselves homeless and at the mercy of the council. All through my life, the walls around me had conspired against me. The first house, with the blue walls, held secrets I could only partially recall. The bungalow in Chard was a real-life house of horrors. In Meare, I had run from the monster. And I had been running ever since. Everywhere I lived, I felt the house had plotted against me. And now, the ultimate irony: I was homeless. My current existence was so precarious, I felt I could quite easily sink without trace. It was one knock after another, some sort of sick joke that my houses played on me. Happiness isn't for me, I told myself miserably. It just doesn't suit me, somehow.

"We've nothing at the moment," the housing officer told me, as I waited in line with my daughters. "The best I can offer is a room in a hotel, while you wait on the list."

With a sinking heart, I agreed. I had no other options. I didn't want to ask Nan, she was elderly and hadn't the space for three extra people. Besides, Lolly had settled in at a new school in Aberystwyth, and I was loath to uproot her again. Our hotel room was small and basic, with twin beds. The girls slept top to toe, I was alongside, and at first, it was fun and cosy as we all three held hands in bed.

"It's just like being on holiday," Lolly smiled.

I thought back to those two caravans, side by side, whilst our home in Chard was being built. It had been such fun – at first. My mind crowded with images of the Nivea moisturiser, my father's rough hands, the clink of his belt. Furiously, I blinked them away. I could not allow this. Not now.

"Yes," I agreed. "It's a sort of holiday. Shall we get fish and chips for supper, as a treat?"

Predictably, as the weeks passed, the novelty faded for us all. I had no money, we had no space and no privacy. All our stuff was packed away in boxes. I found it hard to entertain two small children within the narrow confines of the same four walls, day after day. And yet, I knew, I was fortunate to be on benefits, lucky that we at least had a roof over our heads. Again, the feeling of failure swilled like sludge around my chest. *I am their mother. I am letting them down.* I dragged myself through each neverending day, with no real plan for the next one. When I was at my lowest, Nan, always my guardian angel, swooped in to rescue me.

"You and the girls can stay with me this weekend," she'd say. "In fact, why not leave them with me, and you go and see your pals?"

The Letter

Those occasional breaks, even though I had no money for nights out, were a lifesaver. Nan was my own personal pick-me-up, just as I felt I was sinking into the mud she was there to drag me out. Mum, though she lived far away, did what she could for the girls, too. She invited them to stay during the school holidays and spoiled them just as much as before. But my own relationship with her was as chequered and unpredictable as ever. Just as I felt we were getting on, she'd set me back with a pointed insult or a barbed comment.

"You should have made something of your life by now," she'd tell me.

And though she fussed over the girls, she was often critical of the way I raised them.

"You shouldn't let Lolly have her bottle all day," she told me. "This is why she won't eat her meals. You're too soft."

And again, with the bedtimes.

"They need a routine, Sarah. You should put them to bed earlier."

But it was difficult, with us all sleeping in one room. Mum didn't seem to even consider that. Living at the hotel, with all its stresses, triggered my eating disorder, too. On a practical level, we had no cooker, and we were not allowed to bring in our own food, though sometimes I smuggled in a portion of chips or a pizza for the girls.

The hotel provided breakfast, but it was cereal only, and didn't fill them up for long. My options were either to eat out, or to rely on an invitation from Nan or my aunt. One weekend, I made a deal with the hotel manager to work a couple of hours behind the bar in exchange for the girls and

I eating in the restaurant that night. They loved that, but it was a one-off, and generally mealtimes were tricky. I simply couldn't afford takeaways or restaurants every day. My children were my priority and after they were fed, I picked over what was left. But on a mental level, I didn't want to eat either. The voice was back in my ear, low, menacing and dripping with disgust.

You let him do it, didn't you.

Over time, I starved myself until I was around seven stone. Everyone presumed my weight loss was a direct reaction to my impending divorce.

"You need to eat," Nan urged. "Think of the girls. Think of yourself."

I wanted to eat. But I couldn't. When I began coughing up blood, I was admitted to hospital for tests. For those two weeks, Mum took the girls to her house. And when I was discharged, my dietician insisted I went to stay with a family member, who could help with my recovery.

"Just for a few weeks," she said. "Going back to the same environment, on your own, will be a set-back."

I'd hoped to stay with Mum, but she said:

"I've got the girls here, Sarah. I've got my hands full. You've got yourself in this mess, you need to get yourself out of it."

It was a slap in the face and it was like rewinding back to my childhood, all over again. She appeared to have no time for me, no interest in my recovery. Most significantly, she did not ask what had triggered my illness.

Nan, thankfully, was happy to welcome me. She devised a strict schedule of meals, watching me like a hawk to make sure I finished every last crumb. Breakfast was toast and a mug of tea. Dinner was soup or a chip butty or maybe a slice of homemade pie. Tea was traditionally meat, potatoes and vegetables, a stew or a roast maybe. Supper was toast and a mug of tea again. There was comfort in the cyclical menu, a reassuring predictability.

"Well done, pet," she'd say approvingly, as I forced down my last mouthful.

She was nourishing not only my body, but also my soul, and slowly I gained and maintained weight. One evening, after talking to the girls on the phone, I burst into tears.

"Sorry, Nan," I sniffed, reaching for a tissue. "I just miss them so much."

Nan shook her head angrily and said:

"Your mother should have let you stay with her, so you could be with the children."

It was the only time I ever heard her criticising my mother, and evidently it was a measure of how strongly she felt. It was, in a perverse way, soothing to learn Nan felt a little of my own frustration towards my mother. I didn't feel quite so alone. My aunt visited Nan's one evening, bringing with her a bottle of wine. As she topped up my glass, she said:

"What's behind all the problems, Sarah? Why won't you eat?"

"The divorce, single parenting, the usual stress, you know," I replied lamely. "I'm doing my best."

She looked shrewdly at me.

"I don't believe you," she said. "What's the real problem?"

Perhaps the wine had dulled my sense of danger, because I

heard myself confiding in her, snippets of horror and flashes of terror, surging through from my childhood.

"First my dad, then Stephen," I said quietly.

"No," my aunt gasped, shaking her head. "No. I just don't believe it."

I sighed and took another gulp of my wine. I hadn't expected her to accept it outright, it was a big shock.

But then she said, "Why won't you go to the police? You need to report this. Look, I'll come with you. I'll support you. We need to do something about this."

But it was my turn to shake my head.

"No way," I said. "This has to stay between you and me. My father will kill me. He will kill the whole family if I ever report him. You have to promise me you'll keep quiet."

Nothing she said could change my mind. But though we didn't speak of it again, I noticed she cut all contact with my father and older brother afterwards. And that small concession gave me a feeling of solidarity, as if I had someone on my side.

****

When the month at Nan's was up, the girls came back from Mum's, and we all moved back into the hotel together. I was forcing myself to eat enough to get through the day, but only just. I tried hard to follow Nan's routine, but it was difficult, living in a hotel, and doing it all on my own. My eating disorder seemed to mirror all other aspects of my life, I was on the edge physically, emotionally, financially and psychologically. By the summer of 1997, we had been living in the hotel for almost a year. Frustratingly, though I was still on the waiting list, there were no suitable houses available. The hotel manager was beginning to lose patience, too, with the holiday season in full swing, bookings were flooding in and he wanted our room back for his paying guests.

"I'll do what I can," I promised. "But I have nowhere else to go."

Later that day, I was chatting to my aunt on the phone, and I told her about my latest housing crisis.

"I've got an idea," she said. "We're off to Spain for a fortnight in July, why not come with us? The villa is already paid for. I can cover your flights, my treat. You all need a holiday, and it would get the hotel manager off your back for a while."

"Really?" I gasped. "Oh thank you, you're right, the girls would love to go away."

Those two weeks in Spain were, quite literally, a ray of sunshine in a bleak world. The girls, by now aged eight and three, had a wonderful holiday, and for me, it was a complete escape from the anxiety at home. The underlying worry was always there, but by the pool and on the beach it was so much easier to paint on a smile. When we flew home, there was good news waiting from the council. I was at last being allocated a two-bedroom property.

"A home of our own!" I beamed, as the girls and I danced around the poky hotel room packing our bags.

The new place was a neat two bedroomed newbuild, in a friendly cul-de-sac on a small estate in a village called

Comins Coch, just outside Aberystwyth. The girls shared one bedroom, I had another, and we had a small back garden. There was no furniture at all, and I had nothing left of my own from the house with Andy. Just as I was beginning to wonder how on earth I'd cope, Mum, surprisingly, swung our relationship pendulum back into my favour.

"I can't have my granddaughters living on bare floorboards," she said. "Let me help you."

She drove up from Pembrokeshire a few days later and arranged to take me to a second-hand auction, where I picked out beds and a sofa. Mum paid for them all and she helped me to buy carpets for every room too. I applied for a benefits loan and found a secondhand cooker and washing machine. Slowly, everything was coming together.

"Thanks Mum," I said, as we lugged the sofa up the path. "I do appreciate it."

The house was yet another new start but, much as I was determined to provide stability and security for my daughters, I couldn't shake the feeling that I was doomed and that this was just another temporary stage in my life which would soon be snatched away from me. Each tiny segment of joy seemed destined to end in utter despair.

My divorce was finalised the summer after we moved in, and it was another sharp poke in the ribs – a reminder of my own inadequacies. I had heard nothing more about the sexual abuse claim against my father and assumed the police had taken it no further. But the threat lingered in my thoughts like a sleeping beast. It was only a matter of time, I told myself. Often, my mind was crowded with flashbacks, whizzing past, one after another, like speeding cars. Other times, I felt numb and blank, emptied out and hollow. I hardly knew which was worse. And, in those intrusive flickers of memory, my father became something of a caricature, his mannerisms grotesquely exaggerated, the menacing clink of his belt, the demonic smile, the huge, ham-like hand and the hot, rancid breath on my ear. It was a real-life horror film with my father cast as the villain supreme.

These memories, and the terrors they triggered, only fuelled my conviction that I must stay silent. I was, however, adamant I would never again be at the mercy of the council, or find myself homeless, and I decided to return to education in search of a career. From now on, I was determined to look after us, on my own.

I enrolled at college to study a course in business and administration and after qualifying, I got a part-time office job at the probation service, which I enjoyed. From there, I found work with the Welsh Development Agency, processing reports. In the evenings and at weekends, I cleaned holiday homes, for extra cash. As time went on, I eventually became a supervisor for my department at the Welsh Development Agency and helped to train new staff. My inability to speak Welsh held me back from further promotions, though I understood the language, I couldn't speak it. But I soon devised a system with my clients, who were mainly farmers, where they spoke to me in Welsh, and I replied in English! I worked hard and spent sensibly and was soon able to afford my own car. I picked out a cute yellow VW Beetle, which delighted the girls.

"Our own car!" Lolly grinned.

The car gave us the freedom to go on days out, and to visit Mum and Nan more easily. I booked a holiday to Spain too. A degree of normality was slowly settling upon us, but for how long? How could I live in my present when I was so brutally ensnared by my past?

"I will shoot you. I will shoot you all."

My girls, meanwhile, were growing up and both doing well at school. They were completely different in character. Donna was a tomboy and a daredevil. She loved to play on the big hill outside our home, whizzing down on roller-skates or on her skateboard. One day, she went right under a parked car and was saved from injury only by a quick-thinking passer-by who yanked her out again.

"Donna!" I yelled, tearing down the hill, towards her.

"I'm fine, Mum," she laughed. "I'm gonna try it again."

She reminded me so much of myself on my beloved Fire, being thrown off, into the muck and the puddles, and each time brushing myself down and trying again.

Lolly was quieter and more thoughtful than her little sister, and she preferred being indoors. She loved girly stuff. But when she was excited, or nervous, she would talk very fast, without pausing for breath, her eyes alight. Again, she made me think of myself at her age. I was incredibly proud of them both.

Our household ticked along smoothly most of the time, but there were occasions, inevitably, as a single mother with a full-time job, when my routine came unstuck. One of the girls might be off school with a sore throat or a stomach-ache, and I had to call in a favour from a neighbour, to keep an eye on them while I went to work. It wasn't the end of the world, and besides, I had no choice. But when Mum found out, she was furious.

"You shouldn't be working so much when you have children," she admonished. "You can't farm them out when they're ill. It's not good enough."

"What am I supposed to do?" I asked. "I don't have any family nearby. You live an hour and a half away. I can't take time off work every time the girls are sick, I'd lose my job. And if I don't provide for my kids, who will? I've been homeless once Mum. I won't let it happen again."

Mum tutted, as though the whole thing was my fault and even then, as an adult, she had a way of drilling right through to my core and making me feel I just wasn't good enough. In dismay, I felt like I was back in the corner, with my fingers outstretched, waiting for my father and his belt. Our new and improved relationship was little more than a mirage, I thought sadly. It drew me in, with the promise of reward, only to dissipate and vanish as I got closer.

Though my work was a necessity, to provide for me and the girls, it was also a welcome distraction and a form of therapy. I kept myself busy, all the time, working long hours, running a home, raising my daughters. My aim, not altogether consciously, was to exhaust myself to the point where I had no energy left to think about the abuse and the secrets of my childhood which hung like a noose around my neck. Occasionally, it worked, and I slept well. But most nights I lay awake hour after hour, taunted by demons and the shadows of my past. Memories of the blue bedroom and the hand over my mouth pinballed around my skull. I waited for them to slot into place but agonisingly, they rolled past, far too fast. I sensed the recollections were there, but they were just out of reach.

Alongside this anxiety, my relationships, on all levels, were strained. I loved being a mother, and yet, it was hard work. Some nights, I'd tuck the girls into bed and realise, as I walked downstairs, I had forgotten to kiss them goodnight. Had I told them I loved them? I couldn't be sure. Racked with guilt, I ran back into the bedroom, but this time, the belated hug felt forced and unnatural. Having been starved of affection as a child, I found it hard to show it to my own children. Sometimes, I worried I could feel a palpable distance between us – which was hopefully a product of my imagination – but it distressed me all the same. I recognised shades of my mother in myself, the burying of bad news, the remoteness, the cool reserve. I strived so hard not to be like her, but it seemed the more I tried, the more I failed. The irony was, of course, she was now a wonderful grandmother, showering my children with warmth and love.

Mum had always been very tidy, in part adhering to Dad's strict regime, but she was also inherently houseproud herself. With my own daughters, I'd find myself repeating those same tired lines from my own childhood:

"Only one toy out at once, don't drop bits on the carpet, put those dolls away before your bath."

I didn't want to be obsessively tidy, but I couldn't help it. It was as if the very thing I wanted most to escape was following me around like a bad smell. I simply couldn't shake the shackles of my childhood. The thought of a doll left out on the sofa or a book on the floor was enough to spark my anxiety. Once, when the girls refused to tidy their bedroom, I loaded all their toys into bin bags and hid them in the loft.

"I've thrown them away," I announced. "The binmen took them this morning. Gone for good!"

I caved in when I saw the disappointment on their faces and gave them all back. I had the unenviable task of carting bin bags back down through the loft hatch, balancing on the rickety ladder below. And of course it wasn't a lasting lesson! The girls were tidy for the next few days, before reverting back to being children again. I was the one with the problem, not them. Recognising that was one thing. Solving it was another issue entirely.

Chapter Twenty-Four

I WAS at work one afternoon in 2004, when my phone extension rang and to my surprise – and horror – Stephen was on the line.

"How did you get my number?" I stuttered. "How?"

"Dad wants to see you," he announced, ignoring my question.

"Oh no," I babbled. "No, I can't do that. I'm sorry."

I hadn't seen my father since the girls were small. Lolly was now 15, Donna was 10. Neither of them remembered their grandfather and that was exactly how I wanted it to stay.

"Look, Dad knows where you live and he knows where you work," Stephen said. "Either you arrange to meet him, or he'll just turn up."

A spasm of panic shot through me. Surely not? I had no idea how Dad had this information. I also knew he was not someone to mess around.

"I'll call you back in a minute," I told Stephen. "Just let me make some arrangements."

My eyes filling with frightened tears, I went outside for

some fresh air. When the patrolling security guard noticed I was upset, he handed me a tissue and asked what was wrong.

"If anyone comes to the front desk and asks for me, please call the police," I said. "I'm having some trouble with my family."

Back at my own desk, I called Stephen and made plans to meet Dad in a supermarket café the following day, which was a Saturday. I couldn't risk him turning up at my house, less still at my work. The next morning, as I was getting ready, Lolly said, "I don't want to see him."

"That's fine," I replied. "He's not a nice man at all."

But Donna said, "He doesn't frighten me one bit! I'll come with you, Mum. Keep you safe."

Admittedly, I was frightened of going on my own and hoped Donna's presence might at least make Dad behave more reasonably. But as we walked into the café, I felt my legs giving way. I was so afraid. I was nine years old, all over again, being summoned to my bedroom with a tilt of my father's chin.

"How did you afford that?" my father demanded, nodding towards my yellow Beetle, in the car park.

He hadn't even bothered to say hello, to me or to his granddaughter.

"I work hard," I said, with a sudden burst of defiance. "I work every day of my life. That's how."

My father raised an eyebrow and said, "I wish Stephen was more like you, I really do."

I stared at him. I couldn't believe what I was hearing. Comparing Stephen and I was monstrously inappropriate, surely Dad knew that? And yet despite this – or even because of it – he chose to make his remark. I had no idea if he knew about Stephen's abuse or indeed if Stephen knew about Dad's abuse. Similarly, I hadn't a clue what my mother knew or thought she knew. There was no communication, no bond between each or any of us. The roots of our family were built on quicksand, all of us sinking, some faster than others. Dad and I made stilted conversation for a few moments, but the air was spiked with tension.

"Look, I need to go, I've left Lolly home on her own," I said abruptly.

As we stood up to leave, Dad fished in his pocket and offered me a £10 note. I had a hideous flashback to the sexual assault before the school disco and him pressing a fiver into my small, scared hand. I would not make that mistake again.

"No, I don't want your money," I said sharply.

"I'll have it," Donna piped up, thrilled with the gift, grinning as she stuffed it in her pocket. I couldn't think of a reason for her not to have it. On the drive home, she chattered away about how she might spend her money. But I was mystified, lost in thought. Why had Dad gone to so much trouble to track me down and to see me, after all these years, to then just make a cheap jibe about my car? Likely, he was keeping tabs on me, letting me know what was still at stake, his very presence reminding me of his promise.

"I will shoot you, I will shoot you all."

I was 35 years old, a mother of two, with a good job, a home and a car. And yet, those words struck cold terror into me. I believed them then, just as much as ever.

The Letter

* * * *

My grandad had been ill for some years with emphysema. He'd been a heavy smoker all his life and, in his mid-80s, he now needed oxygen at home to help him breathe. At the start of May 2005, Nan called to say he'd taken a turn for the worse.

"I'll be round there as soon as I can," I promised. "I'm setting off right now."

I took Grandad into hospital, and for the next few days, I visited every evening after work. He was weak and fading, and we knew his time was coming. It was very hard for my daughters, he had been a wonderful great-grandfather, and they thought the world of him. Lolly was due to leave school, her prom was coming up the following month, and Grandad fretted he might not get to see her in her lovely dress.

"I can soon sort that out," she told him. "Don't worry."

The next time she visited, she was wearing her long pale pink prom dress.

"Oh, you look lovely," he beamed, his tired old face lighting up with pride.

One evening later that week, I'd just got home from the hospital when Stephen turned up at my door. I still had no idea how he or Dad had managed to track down my address.

"I've driven from Somerset," he said. "Can I stay here tonight?"

He was with a new girlfriend, his marriage to Dara apparently hadn't worked out. I didn't want a scene on my doorstep but neither did I like the idea of Stephen in my home. The girls were both out on sleepovers, but I couldn't bear the thought of him poking around their bedrooms or sleeping in their beds.

"You'll have to sleep in the living room, on the sofas," I muttered. "Best I can do."

I was dreading having to talk to him, petrified in case he mentioned the rapes, or he referenced the allegation against our father. Inexplicably, I felt I was in the wrong, and I would be the one in trouble if the matters surfaced. Luckily for me, Stephen and his girlfriend spent the evening bickering, and he hardly had time to talk to me.

After I went to bed, I lay awake all night, listening to them arguing. I was too afraid to sleep anyway. I had one eye on the bedroom door and in my mind, I relived the way he had barged through, eyes blazing, flipping me over onto my pink duvet with my legs trapped beneath.

"You breathe a word and I'll say you wanted it."

Even as an adult the overpowering stench of shame clung to me. I thought of the freshly manured field, where Fire had thrown me off before the horse show. I had never truly felt clean since I was a small child, not because of my beloved Fire, but because of my father. The filth was on the inside, and it was impossible to scrub away. So it was a relief, early the following morning, when Stephen left, taking with him the poisonous reminders of our shared past.

On May 18, 2005 Grandad deteriorated sharply, and I rushed to bring Nan to the hospital. He waited for her to arrive and take his hand in hers before he passed away peacefully. They had been married for over 50 years and whilst it broke her heart to lose him, it was a great comfort to me that they had been content for so long.

Mum was at the hospital, and asked if she could stay with me while we planned the funeral.

"It would be nice to spend some time with you and the girls," she said. "I'd like to see what you've done with the house, too."

Again, I was nonplussed by her friendliness, unsure of where it would lead. I was so used to being sidelined, and the physical distance between us had come to symbolise the shortcomings in our relationship.

To my relief, neither Stephen nor Dad came to Grandad's funeral. Grandad was buried in a picturesque little churchyard, which had trees all around and a wooden gate set in the fence. At the graveside, Donna read out a poem that I had written. After the funeral, Nan and I often went to sit with him on sunny evenings. She had a place in the same grave, waiting for her.

"When I'm pushing up daisies and he's driving me mad, I'll jump out and hop right over that gate," she smiled. "Just you wait and see."

Chapter Twenty-Five

FOUR YEARS on from losing Grandad, Mum was struck by a bout of pneumonia, and she ended up in ICU.

I was making the long journey from Aberystwyth to Haverfordwest, several times a week after work, to visit her in hospital. Luckily, she pulled through and was eventually discharged. But her health was still very poor, and I worried something might happen to her. I was so far away, and I feared I might not get there in time. So with mixed emotions, I made the decision to move to Pembrokeshire to be nearer to her. The underlying bitterness was still there, but overlaid was the gratitude I felt towards her as a grandmother. My daughters adored her, she had been the best grandparent they could have wished for, and that easily outshone my own tarnished memories.

"I'm coming to live near you," I told Mum on my next visit. "I want to be closer."

She smiled and squeezed my hand, clearly pleased.

I had anticipated the move would be difficult but, in the end, it all went very smoothly. I got a transfer, through the Housing Association, to Milford Haven, Pembrokeshire. I took redundancy from my job at the Welsh Development Agency and found temporary work at a solicitor's firm near our new home. Lolly was at college and Donna moved schools; both were excited to be nearer their grandmother.

We settled into our new home well and I got friendly with a neighbour, Rita, often popping in for a chat and a brew or a glass of wine after work. One night, after spending some time with Rita, I spotted a 'poke' on Facebook, from someone called Darren Sidebottom. A few days later, he sent a friend request. I had never heard of him, and I was slightly wary. But when I checked his profile, I discovered he was friends with both Rita and her brother, who was in the army and stationed at a base nearby.

"Some weirdo is poking me on Facebook," I said to Rita.

"Oh, he's no weirdo," Rita smiled. "He's single, separated from his wife and he's such a nice bloke. We all know him as Sid."

It turned out Rita's brother was in the same regiment as Darren and between them, they were trying to set us up together. I liked the look of Darren's profile photo and I had to admit, I was flattered. But I'd never really held down a relationship since my divorce, always telling myself I didn't want to fall in love, and I was perfectly content on my own. But in all honesty, partly, I was afraid of failure. I felt I was doomed where men were concerned. And, more than that, I felt I didn't deserve to be happy. I was dirty, damaged, defective. Who on earth would want me? I resolved not to let it go any further. But the following day, there was a message waiting from Darren.

Heard a lot about you, he wrote. *Would be nice to meet up.*

We began messaging regularly, and despite myself, I really liked Darren. He was a typical Yorkshireman, blunt, straight-talking and with a hilariously dry sense of humour. On top of all that, I fancied him like mad. We chatted and flirted over Facebook for a few weeks before I finally agreed to meet him on December 11, 2009. But as our blind date night drew nearer, I had a crisis of confidence.

"Rita, please come with me," I fretted. "What if Darren and I don't get on? What if I've nothing to say? I need some back-up!"

She agreed and roped in her brother and his partner too. When we arrived at the pub, Darren had brought friends with him also, so there was a big group of us. Darren handed me half a lager and lime, and I was so nervous, I gulped it down almost in one go.

"Another one please," I grinned.

Darren grinned back and I knew then, I needn't have worried at all. I felt more comfortable with him than I had with anyone else for years. We chatted all night, swapping stories. Like me, Darren was single, he'd come out of a long-term relationship and had a daughter, Elesha. He was a staff sergeant in the Special Forces Support Group, stationed at a base in South Wales. He'd served in many warzones including Iraq and Afghanistan.

"I'm off to Belize soon on exercise," he told me. "Maybe Afghanistan again after that."

Even though I'd only just met him, I felt a stab of worry. I didn't like to think of him in any danger.

"All part of the job," he said, matter-of-factly.

When the group moved on to another pub, Darren and I lingered behind and shared our first kiss. And from that first date, we were never apart. I invited Darren for Christmas dinner. We'd only been together a couple of weeks, yet he felt like a member of the family. He got stuck in, clearing plates and washing up, like I'd known him for years. On December 27, he flew to Belize, as planned, and I was so downhearted.

"This is something you'll have to get used to, I'm always back and forth," he said, as he kissed me goodbye.

I thought of Harry, and his trips away. But for some reason, I knew this was different. I just knew this was going to last. When he came home, we spent every minute together. And as the weeks passed, on his time off, we had such fun. I was invited to swish army parties where I had to wear ballgowns or cocktail dresses. One evening, I found myself in a grand hall, with candelabras and panelled walls, sitting alongside the army top brass. It was easily the poshest do I'd ever been to. As we took our seats for dinner, a very well-to-do gentleman said to me:

"So, how do you know Sergeant Sidebottom then?"

I hesitated. I didn't know whether 'girlfriend' sounded too casual. Before I could reply, Darren leaned across and said:

"Oh, she's just me weekend bird, you know."

It was like popping a balloon. We all dissolved into helpless giggles, and with that, the tension vaporised. I had the time of my life that night. There was still a lot for me to learn, I wasn't familiar with the etiquette of these occasions and each rule seemed more baffling than the last.

"Only men can buy drinks, only men can pour the port, only ladies can go to the bathroom during the meal," Darren told me. "Don't worry, you'll soon catch on."

It was mind-boggling. But I loved it too, the tradition and the togetherness. At 3am the following morning, we were served with a glass of champagne and a bacon roll.

"Such luxury!" I gasped. "This is my kind of party!"

And despite joking I was his 'weekend bird', Darren treated me like a true princess. We had some wonderful nights with the army. Tragically, in the months to come, some of the new friends I'd made were killed or injured on duty in Afghanistan. My heart went out to their grieving families. And I felt even more afraid for Darren too. I'd found the love of my life, and I was terrified of losing him. But I understood how much he loved his job, and I was so proud when he was promoted to warrant officer.

In our spare time, when he was home, we'd go to scooter rallies. I remembered my little Honda, my first scooter, and I smiled fondly. We travelled all over the UK on mini breaks too. One weekend, we visited London, and as we stood outside Buckingham Palace, Darren said, with a straight face:

"If my boss is home, we could pop in for a brew. I'll check if you like."

I giggled and slipped my arm through his. I realised I'd laughed more since meeting Darren than in the rest of my life. By now, I was working as a document controller and secretary for a construction company. The girls were grown up, with lives of their own. And naturally, as Darren and I became more established, we met each other's families and extended families, and he asked questions about my father and older brother.

"How come you don't see them?" he asked. "Did you fall out?"

"Something like that," I mumbled. "It's complicated really."

The abuse lurked, like a bogeyman, in the background, a circle of dark thoughts chasing around the inside of my head, the repetition leaving me nauseous and anxious. Always, anxious. These unsaid thoughts took up so much space in my head there was no room for anything else, and I was beginning to think that sharing them might help me. In the past, I had sorely regretted confiding in previous partners. Nobody, as yet, had been able to cope with my secret, let alone offer me any support. But I believed, and hoped, Darren would be different.

"I owe you the truth," I told him nervously, as we lay on the sofa one evening after watching a film. "There's a good reason I don't see my father and brother."

Darren's face crumpled with shock and sadness as I told him about the abuse. I didn't share the gruesome details, but I told him I had been raped and sexually abused, right through my childhood.

"My earliest memory is in my father's bedroom with blue walls," I wept. "I can still feel his hand over my mouth. I don't even know what happened to me that night. But the fear will live with me until I die."

"I'm so sorry," he said softly.

"Look, I understand if you want to finish things," I said, gulping back my tears. "It's a lot to process. I get it. Walk away if you like."

"No," Darren replied firmly. "Never. You can count on me, Sarah. I want you to report this, I want us to go to the police, together."

I shuddered at the thought.

"My father will shoot me," I told him. "He will shoot us all. You have no idea what kind of monster he is. I really can't say a word outside this house."

"I can protect you," Darren promised. "He won't hurt you, not whilst I'm here."

But I couldn't risk it. Darren offered to speak to his friend, who was a police officer, for some advice.

"Anonymously," I insisted. "Don't tell him my name. I don't want to be linked to this in any way."

But when Darren was ready to make the call, I backed out. I was just too scared.

"We'll do this in your own time," Darren conceded. "But when you're ready, I will be ready too."

Chapter Twenty-Six

FOR SO many years, I had felt as if I'd been treading water, sometimes swallowing huge mouthfuls of sludge, my head dipping dangerously under the surface. Many times, my lungs had filled, and I had almost drowned. But with Darren by my side, I was suddenly on dry land. He'd pulled me out, rescued me, and was leading me to safety.

The weight of the abuse remained, as always. But Darren was shouldering it alongside me, and sharing my burden made it almost bearable. Over the summer of 2011 there was more good news when Lolly gave birth to a little girl, my first grandchild. I was delighted. Nan and Mum were over the moon, too. Now, we had five generations of eldest females in the family. It was quite an achievement, and the local newspaper got in touch with Lolly to see if they could run a story.

"What do you think, Mum?" she asked.

"It's a lovely idea," I told her. "I'll get everyone together."

That August, the article ran in the weekly paper, with the headline: *Daughters lead the way across five generations.* There was a photo of Nan, Mum, me, Lolly, and her new baby. I had been excited to see our story in print, but when I picked up a copy of the newspaper, I felt a lump in my throat. The picture of the smiling faces, looking back at me, seemed like such a sham. The idea of a strong female line, of women leading the way in our family, was so tragically misplaced. My mother had suffered domestic abuse. I lived in fear of both my father and older brother, we were battered, bullied and controlled in the worst ways possible.

Mothers and daughters will always share a special bond… read the article. My mother was quoted, saying: "We're a very tight-knit family and we try to get together as often as we can… we have such a deep-rooted history…"

I was pleased for Lolly, the article was a lovely keepsake for her. But we were not a happy family. And we were not a close family. We were a family sitting on a wasps' nest of lies and secrets. And when the nest exploded, the shock of all those stings might well tear us apart forever.

Special bond with my mother? I said to myself in disbelief. *There is hardly any bond at all.*

By the time the article was published, Nan was in very poor health. She had been diagnosed with dementia some months previously and had become very forgetful and vacant. Often, she did not recognise me at all. Sometimes, she would confuse me and my mother, another caustic reminder of how similar we both were. She was in and out of hospital but always rallying to come home after a few days. We knew she could not carry on for much longer. In October 2011, I had booked a weekend to Butlins with a few girlfriends and while

The Letter

I was away, Nan was taken into hospital again. In concern, I called her on the ward.

"I will be home soon. Enjoy your holiday and I'll see you when you get back," she told me.

But that weekend, before I could make it home, she passed away. Even though I had been preparing myself for her death, it shook me to my soul. Nan had been everything to me and, without knowing, she had pulled me through the worst of the abuse and the very lowest points of my childhood. She had been a mother, a grandmother and a best friend to me. The only person in my life who had loved me as a child should be loved. My grief ruptured inside me like a bursting dam as my tears flowed.

At her funeral, I read a poem I had written myself, and afterwards she was buried with Grandad, in the churchyard with the little gate. Her words came back to me and, despite myself, I smiled.

When I'm pushing up daisies and he's driving me mad, I'll jump out and hop right over that gate.

"Oh, I wish you could, Nan," I said softly. "I'd give anything to see you one last time."

* * * *

Four months after Nan's death, Darren was posted to Belize on exercise. We relied on emails as the most efficient way of staying in touch. One morning, I opened my laptop to discover he had sent me the lyrics from our favourite Madness song, 'It Must Be Love'.

I never thought I'd miss you, half as much as I do. And I never thought I'd feel this way, the way I feel about you…

I beamed; an infusion of joy running right from my toes to the top of my head. Not for the first time, I appreciated just how happy he made me. Without stopping to think it through, I emailed back quickly.

Would you like me to be your life-long partner?

It was 2012, and a leap year after all, so traditionally I was allowed to propose! Even so, my heart skittered as I logged off. All day, I kept checking my laptop and snapping it shut in annoyance when there was no reply. There was a six-hour time difference between the UK and Belize, and I also knew Darren didn't get much time to access emails, so I'd simply have to be patient. No news was not necessarily bad news. Two days on, his typically understated reply landed in my inbox at last.

Suppose so, yes…

I whooped out loud and, though I was home alone, I danced around the bedroom with my hands in the air. It was official. We were getting engaged. When Darren got home, we celebrated and he took me out to choose a beautiful ring, a diamond at the centre surrounded by smaller diamonds. Neither of us were in any rush and we settled on a long engagement, especially since Darren was away so much. But later that year I slipped at work, damaging my right knee badly and needing surgery for a complete knee replacement.

"I'm not going away again and leaving you on your own," Darren said. "You can hardly walk."

He was ready for a fresh challenge too, and we wanted

to spend more time together, especially during my recovery. And so, late in 2012, Darren left the army and trained as a gas engineer. It was a new chapter and exciting for us both.

We began house-hunting in Barnsley, South Yorkshire, where Darren's family lived, and soon found the perfect home, a cosy semi-detached on a friendly street. The moment I walked in through the front door, I knew this was the place for us.

"You're going to love it here," Darren said. "I can just tell. And your father has no idea where you are, so don't worry. He'll never track you down."

But even as he spoke, a chilling image of the guns was blasted onto my retinas. He would find me anywhere, I was in no doubt about that. And when he did, he would kill me.

We settled in well in Barnsley and bought a touring caravan. Darren quickly got to know other army veterans in the town and at the Remembrance Day parade, the following year, he was introduced to the founder of a charity called Help 4 Homeless Veterans. The organisation offered practical and emotional support for homeless veterans.

"They've asked me to become a trustee," he said. "What do you think?"

Immediately, my mind went back to Nan and Grandad, and the charity work they'd done for many years through the British Legion. Shortly before Grandad became ill, they'd been invited to Buckingham Palace, in recognition of their contribution to the community, and had the best day out ever. It felt somehow that this new charity, this chance, was a sign from Nan. She was sending a nudge for us both to get involved and offer our support.

"I think it's a great idea," I smiled. "I'll help out too."

Whilst Darren was involved with the running of the charity, I began fundraising. I organised raffles at work and at home, badgering local businesses to make donations as prizes, and persuading my colleagues and friends to buy raffle tickets. I loved to keep busy, the fundraising was a distraction from my own problems. Besides, the army had given us both so much, and it was satisfying to give a little back.

Life was finally feeling good.

Chapter Twenty-Seven

EARLY IN 2019, I picked up the phone to a police officer. Before he had even finished introducing himself, I sensed this was it; the moment I had dreaded and longed for all my life was finally here.

My skin prickled with an expectation so intense, I could barely hold the phone. There was no need for explanation. No need for him to speak at all. I knew this call was about my father.

"There has been a complaint of sexual abuse against your father," he told me. "We are contacting you to ask if you have been a victim also?"

Even though I had predicted it, the words hit me like a hammer. Reeling, I sank into the nearest chair. I thought of the Nivea. I thought of the guns. I thought of the belt. I thought of the pain. Most of all, I thought of the fear. The blinding, biting, blazing fear.

There was no way I could speak out, none at all. Yet I heard myself say:

"Yes, I will give a statement. Please can we arrange a date?"

The officer promised to call me back. When Darren found out, he was ecstatic.

"I knew you could do this," he told me. "I knew it. I am so proud of you."

I wasn't quite sure what had sparked the about-turn in my mind. But knowing there must be other victims – because the police had told me there were other complaints – had really swayed me. I had to support those people, even if I could not support myself. A strong sense of purpose surged within me, to make sure others did not suffer as I had.

At first, I was on tenterhooks, waiting for a call from the police to arrange a date for my statement. In preparation, I bought myself a small hard-backed red book and recorded memories and flashbacks as they resurfaced. At first, the outer layer of my mind was hard and unyielding, like a frozen pond. But once I had broken through, the recollections poured out. It was like turning over stones, with a new and unsightly memory wriggling and writhing under each pebble. Each one appeared to summon the arrival of the next, as if my traumas were waiting in a queue, bursting to get out.

"I think this might be good for me," I told Darren, as I scribbled page after page. "I've kept this information to myself for far too long."

But the days passed and slowly smudged into weeks, and I heard nothing from the police. With nearly 50 years having elapsed since the abuse began, I worried perhaps it was all too long ago and there was no reasonable chance of a conviction after all. Maybe I had left it all too late? From spending my whole life fearing the abuse being uncovered, now, conversely, I wanted it exposed. I was committed to seeing this all the way through to a criminal trial.

"Don't worry, the police will be in touch," Darren assured me. "It just takes time."

But winter turned to spring, and still there was no update. Even Darren began to have doubts. I oscillated between fear, frustration and anger. How could they just leave me, in limbo, month after month? I had finally gathered my courage, finally confronted my darkest demons, and the police were not interested. That was how it seemed to me. In July that year, almost seven months on, and quite out of the blue, the call finally came.

"I'm so sorry," an officer said. "Your file was misplaced. I've just been looking through this case and we would like to take a statement from you."

The date he had set for the interview was Lolly's 30th birthday.

"No," I said quickly. "I can't do that. We'll have to make it later please."

Late in August 2019, Darren and I travelled to Pembrokeshire, where the investigation team was based. We had arranged to stay with Mum, but I was under strict instructions from the police not to talk about the case with her, as she would most probably be called as a witness at the trial.

"You could prejudice the trial if you discuss it with anyone at all," I was told. "Best to keep it all to yourself."

Even so, I was strangely apprehensive at the prospect of facing Mum. Now she knew something of what I had been through, how would she behave towards me? Just below my thought line was a niggle that maybe she would blame me, and she would see me as a curse and a jinx, in the same way I had always seen myself. In my daydreams, I allowed myself to imagine her throwing her arms around me and apologising for all those years I had been let down. But that was foolish and naive. I knew my mother better than that. There was very little chance of her saying sorry.

However, when she answered the door, she wrong-footed me yet again. She welcomed me in as if nothing at all was wrong, as if this was just a standard family visit. She showed no signs of shock or stress, and she did not reference the case in any way. Neither did she ask how I was coping. A hug, a kiss, an apology – I had hoped for all or any. It was no surprise that I received none of these. But it broke my heart, nonetheless.

I appreciated, outside of my own turmoil, that Mum may well be upset herself. Her ex-husband and eldest son had been accused of the worst possible crimes, under her own roof, against her own daughter.

"How are you?" I asked her, but she waved my question away, as if I was an irritating fly. She didn't bother asking me how I was.

As the time of my police interview drew nearer, my nerves began rattling.

"I can't do this," I gasped. "I can't do it."

Mum stood in front of me but did not even make eye contact. All that we could not say hung in the air between us, dense and awkward. And then, wordlessly, she turned and walked into another room. Chris, my stepfather, put his arms around me, and said:

"Sarah, you can do this. You need to do this. You are stronger than you think."

I was so choked. I could not even find the words to thank him. His encouragement was just what I needed at that moment, his kindness and support touched my injured soul. I wished it could have been Mum. I wished she could have been there for me. But, as was the painful pattern of our lives, she was not.

That afternoon I gave two interviews, firstly in a local police station, and then at a specialist suite, where I spoke to trained officers and my account was video recorded. By the time I got back to Mum's at nearly 6pm, flanked by two officers, I was drained. Every last drop of energy squeezed from me. I might as well have been in a boxing match, I felt so bruised and broken. Yet I felt strangely light too, positive and optimistic, as though a load had been lifted. I had said it all out loud for the first time ever. I had included my father and my brother, and every single detail I could remember. I left nothing out. And though it was like opening old wounds and watching the fresh blood flow, I knew, instinctively, I had done the right thing.

As we walked back into the house, my legs barely able to support my exhausted frame, Mum met me in the hallway.

"Why did you have to take so long?" she snapped.

I was dumbfounded. I couldn't believe that timing was her main priority. How could she be so insensitive and cruel? And that, it transpired, was her only comment on the whole day, and it encapsulated much of what was wrong between us. All my life, I had tried and failed to pluck up courage to confide in my mother about the abuse. Now she finally knew, and she seemed, if anything, exasperated with me.

"You've been through a lot today," the police officer told me. "You did really well."

I nodded gratefully. I only wished my own mother felt the same. The officer stressed once again, before he left, how we must not discuss the case with anyone while the CPS considered potential charges against my father and Stephen. I understood that completely. But these rules did not prevent my mother from hugging me, from asking me how I was, or from saying sorry. These rules did not prevent her showing me love. I did not blame her for the abuse. But increasingly, I blamed her for not supporting me through it.

* * * *

Now that the investigation was real, it was time for me to confide in my daughters. They had always known there was something wrong at the heart of my family, and they understood there was a specific problem with my father. But nothing could have prepared them for the truth. I did not share any details, but the revelation of the abuse was, in itself, distressing.

"Mum, this explains why you are the way you are," Donna said.

Her comment was like a piano chord, striking sadness right through me. What would I have been like if I wasn't abused? What kind of mother would I have been? A better one, certainly. I asked myself this question almost every day, in different contexts, and now Donna had prompted it too. Would I have done well at school, pursued the creative career I always dreamed of? Would I have been more confident, more stable? I felt sure my relationships would have been smoother. What kind of person could, or should, I have been? More pertinently, I could have been one whole woman, instead of splitting myself chronically and diametrically into two. The other Sarah, and myself. Always at odds with each other.

For a couple of months after my police interview, I heard nothing. Then in October 2019, I was told a new investigating officer had been assigned.

"Why?" I asked. "I put my trust into the last officer. Why can't he see the case through?"

But that apparently wasn't possible. Next, I learned the case was to be handed to Avon and Somerset police. The investigation would have to begin all over again.

"No way," I said. "I'm not going through it all again. Please don't do this to me."

To my relief, the new officer agreed with me. The weeks passed, and there was nothing to report. Mum was interviewed, as a witness for the prosecution, though my information came through the police and not from her.

Every two weeks, I called or emailed the officers, asking for an update. But if I heard anything back, it was usually just a quick email to say there was no progress. I understood investigations took time, but this seemed so frustratingly slow.

The days dragged and, with the case hanging over me like a guillotine, I could think of nothing else. In my interview, I'd told the police everything, right back to those patchy memories of the blue bedroom, the hand over my mouth, the scratchy beard on my cheek. The officers had made it clear they believed my account was credible. But they had also warned me it was all so long ago, and there was little evidence. They explained I would be easily discredited under cross-examination, because I had been so young. It was my word against his. Throughout my early childhood, the assaults in the caravan and in the stables, my memories were much clearer. But still, I could not give exact dates and times. I had no witnesses. There had been so many attacks, they had, in many instances, all blurred into one. My whole childhood felt like one interminable, intolerable, assault. But again, it was my word against his.

As the weeks went by, I began to wonder whether the case would be dropped, and whether I had wasted my time. I had started this whole process in support of the other unknown victims who had come forward against my father. But now, I wanted justice for me, too. I had stayed quiet for 50 years and it was already way too long. I felt like grabbing a megaphone and yelling out of my bedroom window:

"My father is a paedophile! He should be in prison!"

Yet alongside this nascent resolve, I was jittery with terror. Dad and Stephen had been arrested, interviewed and released, so they now knew I had spoken out against them. They could track me down if they chose to. Would my father come for his revenge, as he had always promised? I became more apprehensive and afraid than ever before, checking and double-checking my windows and doors, screening my calls, refusing to answer the front door.

One winter morning, I called the police for a routine update, and as the officer chatted, he said:

"Obviously it's a setback with your mother pulling out."

"What?" I replied. "Pulling out of what?"

"Your mother has withdrawn her co-operation, she will no longer agree to be a prosecution witness," he said. "I'm sorry, Sarah. I thought you knew."

In the silence that followed, I was yanked right back almost five decades, to my childhood. There I was, quivering in the corner, with my fingers outstretched, waiting for my father's belt. Now, as then, my own mother had washed her hands of me. When the chips were down, she had simply looked the other way.

After the call ended, I cried my heart out. What hurt even more was that she hadn't bothered to tell me of her decision herself. I had no idea why she had pulled out, no idea why she had left it to the police to drop the bombshell. Her physical health was poor, but as a mother myself, I knew I'd rather be wheeled into court on my deathbed than let my daughter down. My own view is my mother was concerned about how she might be portrayed in court; panicked that her parental shortcomings would finally be exposed. And so, as was her way, she put herself before me. She let me down catastrophically and this occasion seemed to hurt more than many others before it.

In my mind, her support at the trial was her final chance

of redemption as a mother, and she had flung it back in my face. Days afterwards, with my self-belief at rock bottom, I found myself emptying the bathroom cabinet, swallowing as many pills as I could cram into my mouth. When Darren came home from work, he heard me vomiting into the toilet and rushed to help.

"Don't worry, I'm here now," he said, gathering up the empty pill packets around me. "You're going to be OK."

Gently, he carried me downstairs, and rushed me to hospital. Sick and disorientated, my mind's eye was clouded with memories of my teenage overdose, and hazily, I compared my mother's reaction, or rather the lack of it, with Darren's. The bathroom floor was covered with empty packets of pills, yet she hadn't even bothered to ask me about them or to call a doctor. She had never once asked if or why I had swallowed all those tablets. Darren, however, was beside himself with worry, holding me close and reassuring me as we waited to be seen in A&E. And yet the disparity was all part of the problem. My mother had never been there for me. I struggled to come to terms with my father's abuse. But I also struggled to cope with my mother's rejection.

"I just don't want to be here anymore," I told Darren wearily. "I've really had enough. I'm sorry."

I was referred for mental health help but warned the waiting list was long.

In the days afterwards, Darren did his best to cheer me up and, as Christmas approached, I tried hard to act and feel a little brighter. December marked our anniversary, 10 wonderful years since we had met. On Christmas morning,

The Letter

Darren handed me a white envelope. Inside, I was intrigued to find an official looking document, made out to Mrs Sarah Sidebottom.

"I've bought you a private registration for your car," he announced. "It's your initials followed by SYD, my nickname. And it belongs to Mrs Sarah Sidebottom which means…"

"Which means we're getting married!" I whooped, throwing my arms around him. "I am so lucky to have you."

We had never got around to setting a date before, but by the time New Year came around, we had everything arranged. Just as we were counting down the days, Covid hit, and our wedding had to be postponed. As with many thousands of others, our plans went on indefinite hold. Mum was disappointed, she had already bought herself a new dress and fascinator, for the occasion.

"I was looking forward to seeing you both married," she said.

"Don't worry, Mum, we'll rearrange it," I promised.

I'd resolved to push my court case aside, so we could all enjoy the wedding. I accepted I could not address Mum's decision to withdraw as a prosecution witness, however hurt I felt. But I knew my time would come, after the conclusion of the trial. Until then, I vowed to say nothing at all. I'd even bought Mum a champagne glass, with her name engraved, as a 'mother of the bride' gift.

I'd asked Chris to give me away and had chosen a silver pocket watch for him. Over the years, he had been more of a dad to me than my own father ever had. My daughters had bought new dresses too. We had put so much thought and planning into our big day and I couldn't wait. But we kept having to rearrange, one new date after another, sending out new invites and new plans, as the Covid regulations changed.

In July 2020, Mum suffered a heart-attack and was fitted with a pacemaker. She was diagnosed with emphysema too. Her health, already fragile, had deteriorated since the police investigation had started – but I was unsure whether her stress was triggered by concern for me, or for herself. I did not dare ask, knowing I may not get an answer I liked.

By September 2020, Darren and I both decided enough was enough. We had been waiting so long to get married and it seemed there was no end in sight to the Covid restrictions.

"I don't really care who's there, as long as we are," Darren told me. "I just want you to be my wife."

I felt exactly the same. Because of the restrictions on guest numbers, we couldn't decide who to invite. So we opted to get married on our own, at short notice, in secret. I arranged to live-stream the wedding to Mum, and she promised to get dressed up in her outfit and fascinator, just as if she was at the ceremony. I could not deny her that.

The night before our big day, I made my own wedding cake. And as I cracked the eggs and weighed out the sugar, the years unspooled and I heard Nan's lilting Welsh voice, over my shoulder:

"Get the mixture nice and fluffy before you put the eggs in, love."

The memory was so strong, I was tempted to turn and bury my face in her apron, drinking in her Lily of the Valley scent. I missed her so much. As I spooned the cake into the tin, I heard her murmuring in approval.

"Looks nice, love, remember the needle test, make sure it's cooked through."

"Will do," I beamed. "I learned from the best, Nan. I really did."

Darren and I were married in our local community hall, with two pals as witnesses. I wore an off-the-shoulder full length dress in white silk. Darren was handsome and smart in a new suit. A meal was arranged by two friends Lisa and Dylan who made our wedding – the best man and his wife.

"You look beautiful," he smiled.

Afterwards, we enjoyed a glass of bubbly and a slice of wedding cake. And then we set off on honeymoon, to the Lake District, in our touring caravan. There was hardly anyone there, very few pubs, hotels or shops were open, but that didn't bother us one bit. I was overjoyed to be married to the love of my life, at last.

After we returned home to reality, I picked up a chest infection, which lingered for weeks. When I began coughing up blood, Darren persuaded me to go to A&E for advice. And whilst I was waiting to be seen, I passed out, and was admitted to hospital. Because of Covid restrictions, Darren wasn't allowed to visit. He wasn't even permitted to bring me any fresh clothes. On a lonely ward, I tested positive and then negative for Covid. I was already battling anxiety and claustrophobia and wearing a face mask made it worse than ever. I had blood tests, chest X-rays and CT scans, which again triggered my claustrophobia. One doctor thought I had a blood clot. Another blamed my symptoms on pneumonia. Because of lockdown, the hospital was overstretched, and the administration was chaotic, and by the time I came home, I still did not have the results of my scans.

"I need to find out what's wrong with me," I told Darren.

I was conscious both Grandad and Mum had emphysema and worried I might be affected too. I called the hospital to request a copy of my latest CT scan, along with the results.

To my surprise, just two weeks later, I received an email containing all my medical records.

Chapter Twenty-Eight

"THEY'VE SENT the whole lot by mistake," I told Darren, as I checked my emails. "I'll just have to print them off and sift through them all."

Darren offered to help and made us both a brew, as the printer began spitting out sheets of paper. I was busy leafing through records of my pregnancies, pausing on long-forgotten details of my post-natal care, when suddenly Darren's face bleached.

"Sarah," he said, his hand shaking a little. "You need to look at this letter."

My heart was thudding as he placed the paper in front of me. The letter was dated 25 April 1973, a few days after my fourth birthday, written from one doctor to another, about me. As I began to read, time and space fell away. And all those years of terrifying flashbacks and confusing slivers of memory slotted sickeningly into place:

Your patient (Miss Sarah Bowditch) was admitted under the surgeons having fallen downstairs and landed on a go-cart handle which tore her perineum. She was examined under a general anaes-

thetic and it was found that the posterior wall of the vagina was torn up to the fornix. The perineum was also torn, together with the bottom 3cms of the rectum. This was repaired exactly as one would a 3rd degree tear, with catgut to the rectum and subcuticular dexon to the skin. She was given one pint of blood as it was felt she had lost a fair bit. She did well post-operatively and was discharged on the 19.04.73. She will be seen in out-patients. It is of course very important in cases such as this to keep an open mind as to the cause of the injury, but we feel in this case that the parents' story is the correct one.

Around me, my living room dissolved, all the colours running into one another like a paint palette under a running tap. My blood screeched to a halt in my veins, frozen mid-flow, with sharp icicles jabbing at the backs of my eyes.

"Sarah? Are you ok, love?"

Darren's voice was faint, muffled into the background, as though he was stuck down a long tunnel. I was vaguely aware my legs were stinging, scalded by my coffee; I had dropped it without even noticing. This letter was a fireball, a grenade, right into my soul. It was at once shocking and yet entirely expected. For here, after 50 years, was the explanation and proof of my earliest trauma in the blue bedroom.

I had no memory of going into hospital, no recollection at all of the surgery or of my recovery. But without doubt, I knew these horrific injuries, which had ripped me apart, had been caused not by a go-cart, but by my father raping me. Strangely, although I was repulsed and shattered, there was also a tinge of relief, running through me. At last, I knew. At last, those snippets of horror made sense. Again I saw myself, walking downstairs, with the blood dripping down my legs as my mother and father argued in the hallway. Snapped back to the present, I heard myself wailing.

"My mother," I cried. "She must have known. Surely, she must have known."

Even given her past history of half-truths and cover-ups, I was appalled she had kept this from me. The memories crowded in, and I saw myself giving birth to Lolly, and the midwife asking if I'd ever had a blood transfusion.

"Oh yes," Mum said casually, contradicting my earlier reply.

Back then, I'd been so focussed on my labour pains, I'd just nodded and forgot to ask Mum about it afterwards. But even if I had, she would just have brushed it away. Closed the book, as always. Yet here it was, in black and white, solid proof of her complicity.

She was given one pint of blood.

"She must have known," I sobbed again.

My pain was as red and as raw as a skin graft. I read and reread the letter, each word like a punch, and the last line cutting me right to the core.

…we feel in this case that the parents' story is the correct one.

The use of the plural was a further twist of the knife, that tiny apostrophe was the confirmation I did not want, that my mother had lied, to save my father. And even with them both sticking to the same story, I could not understand why the doctors had accepted it.

"Why did they believe my parents?" I protested. "I was already known to police because of the domestic abuse. I was known to social services as well because I had been in and out of care. Why did nobody investigate this? Why?"

The cold irony was that my father would never have allowed a go-cart into the house. Outside toys had to stay outside, that was one of *his rules*. From my memory, we didn't even have a go-cart, Stephen and I would have been far too young to ride one. His cover story was feeble, but then, he probably hadn't bothered putting any effort into it, and why would he? He thought he could get away with anything, and he was right about that. His 'story' was accepted without question.

Darren was frantically skimming through the rest of my records, but there was nothing else which referred to my injuries. It appeared I'd had no aftercare and no follow-up appointments, save the single trip to out-patients which was mentioned in the letter, and I had no proof I'd ever even attended that. I had just been left to cope with the most appalling internal damage.

"How could they leave a small child with such serious internal injuries?" I cried, a seam of fizzing fury scorching right through me. "I was ripped to pieces inside. Why did nobody check on me?"

I had been so badly let down by doctors and social services. But more, by my own mother, and mostly, by my beast of a father. My family was riddled with lies. Like woodworm, each time I opened a drawer or a cupboard, I'd find another infestation. The final degradation in the letter was almost lost in the detail and was, in its way, more painful than anything else: I had been released from hospital on 19 April 1973 – the day of my fourth birthday.

The Letter

With my head in my hands, I wept for my three-year-old self, physically and mentally ripped to pieces by the very man who should have loved and protected me. He had put me into foster care on my second birthday. And he had put me in hospital for my fourth birthday. Recently, the police had asked me to make my statement on my daughter's birthday. It felt like someone, or something, was intent on snatching away each scrap of happiness I found. I knew then, I would never celebrate another birthday for the rest of my life.

And yet, even as I cried, I understood this letter represented precisely what had been missing: concrete proof. Now, I had solid medical evidence which linked directly to my allegations that my father had raped me. It was a mystery why a letter from 1973 had somehow got mixed up in my 2020 medical records. And so while fate might have a hand in bringing me down, there was also someone firmly on my side too. An image of my Nan, smiling, her hands covered in flour, twinkled suddenly in my mind. She was looking out for me. She'd sent me this letter, I felt sure of it. For although it was a firebomb, it was also a priceless gift.

Chapter Twenty-Nine

THAT SAME afternoon, I emailed the police with my discovery, and was surprised when my phone rang almost immediately in response.

"This letter is the golden nugget in your case," the officer told me. "This is exactly what we needed."

As was my way, I was conflicted; delighted one minute, despairing the next. The letter unearthed so many buried secrets that it was impossible for me to focus on any single thread.

But I found myself, time after time, returning to my mother's treachery, pulling at my thoughts until they unravelled into a large, knotted mess. She had known about my hospital admission, the surgery, and the blood transfusion. Had my father terrified her into staying quiet and forced her into corroborating his flimsy cover story about the go-cart? Had she worked out or suspected the sordid truth behind his lies? If not, how on earth did she think I had come by my injuries? Had they, and this thought was unbearable, concocted their story together?

The Letter

It burned that I couldn't ask her about any of this because I was forbidden from discussing the case with her. I had to accept I would simply have to wait to confront her until after the trial. Under my skin, my anger seethed and hissed, as though my blood itself was boiling. How could she let me down like this? How could she turn a blind eye? The tapeworm of resentment which had snaked right through my life seemed to burst out for air. It felt like the ultimate betrayal. The final reckoning.

The truth was out in the open yet, ironically, I was not allowed to say a word. All my life I'd put other people first, and not once had they done the same for me. With the exception of Nan, nobody had ever really considered me. My father had raped me from the age of three onwards. My mother had never once taken my side. I had tried to save her life by staying quiet, when all along, she was hiding a grotesque secret of her own. I was angry, yes. But worse than that, I was sad. Unspeakably sad. Looking back, I do not think my mother was a liar, but neither do I think she was truthful. The difference is at once subtle and momentous.

When I finally got around to reading the remainder of my medical records, to check my recent scans, I discovered I had mild emphysema and pneumonia. I was prescribed inhalers and my health, physically at least, improved.

Stephen and my father were charged with a string of rapes and sexual assaults against several children, of whom I was one. I had been holding out hope that they would plead guilty, knowing deep down it was a fantastical wish, yet was nonetheless dismayed when they did not. And, to add to my dismay, after their magistrates' appearance, I learned they had been granted bail without any travel restrictions in place.

"How is that fair?" I asked furiously.

The perpetrators were subject to no travel restrictions whilst I, the victim, was under siege in my own home, bombarded, minute by minute, with threats from my past. Apart from going to work, I rarely left the house. I had a panic alarm fitted and Darren and I paid to have CCTV installed, inside and out.

"When I'm at work, I'll check in with you, every hour," he promised.

Even then, I didn't feel safe. I could not sleep, could not eat, could not function properly. Some days, I was unable to drive because of panic attacks. Other times, I couldn't walk down the street for fear of someone running up behind and attacking me. In crowds, I would become dizzy and panicky, unable to overcome the feeling of being hemmed in.

Darren and I had bought tickets for a UB40 concert, but when we arrived, I was overpowered by the sheer numbers in the audience and suffered a panic attack.

"I'll have to go home," I said to Darren breathlessly. "I'm sorry."

I felt so guilty, ruining his night, as well as my own. Deep down, a slimy slither of doubt taunted me that Darren might not put up with me for much longer. And I would not have blamed him. I didn't want to put up with myself either. But despite everything, Darren remained strong and loyal and my love for him only deepened.

"It's just a concert," he soothed. "We can see them another time. No big deal."

On another occasion, he took me out shopping. I had bitten the inside of my mouth during anxiety attacks, and needed mouth ulcer gel. But as I waited in the queue to pay, with the tube in my hand, I felt the breath of another customer on the back of my neck and I froze in alarm. I was trembling so much, I ran from the shop and let Darren take my place in the queue.

"I'm sorry," I gasped, when he found me leaning against a wall outside.

After I had calmed down, he insisted on buying me some new clothes.

"It'll cheer you up," he said.

I managed to make my way through a shop and pick out a couple of dresses. But in the changing rooms, I looked in the mirror and saw only my damaged soul staring back at me. I couldn't focus on the clothes at all. And as I drew back the curtain, ready to leave, I was confronted by the faces of my abusers superimposed onto all the other customers in the waiting room. Screaming in horror, I fled, leaving my new dresses behind.

"Don't worry," Darren reassured me. "We can try again, another day."

But everywhere I went, I seemed to see my father's face. My mind played cruel tricks and I convinced myself I spotted him outside the local shop or in the park. These fears were at once irrational and completely real. I alone knew what he was capable of, and carrying this oppressive responsibility on my own was hard.

I wished, desperately, for a remote control to simply switch my thoughts off. More than anything, I needed one moment of peace. At night, in fitful dreams, I visualised the Nivea tub, the brown belt and the meaty hand, tangible instruments of torture, the backdrop to my miserable childhood. I stared into the bottomless black of my father's eyes and I was again paralysed by pain, fear, and hopelessness. In the dream, his eyes morphed into a huge black hole, a waiting tomb, and it took all my strength not to throw myself into it. The following morning, the remnants of my nightmares hung around me like a toxic fog, trailing in my wake. I could never truly shake them off.

After the charges were brought, the investigation seemed to slow to a halt once more. I called the officers every two weeks but there was rarely much to report. I felt like I was a nuisance, pestering the team, who issued the standard response each time I called.

"No, Sarah, no updates, sorry."

Mother's Day came in Spring 2021, and it stuck in my throat as I chose a card in the local newsagents. With this painful chasm between us, this glaring lack of truth and transparency, how could we celebrate Mother's Day, as if we were a normal mother and daughter?

"Happy Mother's Day," I said brightly, choosing to make a phone call rather than visit her in person. Even to me, my voice sounded brittle and fake. If Mum spotted it, she never mentioned it. She was, after all, good at not hearing and seeing things. Her health, meanwhile, deteriorated once again and in November 2021, she was admitted to hospital with breathlessness. One morning on my way to work, I managed to catch her on the phone, as she was waiting for a CT scan.

"I can hardly get my breath," she wheezed.

"Don't talk," I soothed. "Save your energy. I'll see you soon. Let me know the results of the scan please, won't you?"

I envisaged her nodding, and then she said, so softly I might have missed it:

"You do know I love you, Sarah."

My heart welled with a curious mixture of sadness, joy and regret. The letter loomed large in my mind, like a shadow across the sun. But this was not the time to challenge her.

"I love you too, Mum," I replied.

That same week, I got a call to say Mum had been put on end-of-life care in hospital.

"I'm on my way," I said. "I'll pack the car and set off."

But before I could even begin my journey, I picked up a second call to say she had passed away. She was 73 years old. I was grief stricken, sad for all that we had shared, sadder still for all we had not shared. And in a hammer blow, I realised the secrets of my surgery, aged three, had died with her. I would never now be able to ask her for the truth.

"Oh Mum," I said sadly. "You've left such a mess behind."

There was so much I needed to say to her after the trial and it had been building inside me, like a river about to burst its banks. I had hoped to talk to Mum about the abuse, ask her what she knew, when and how. I had planned to challenge her decision to withdraw as a prosecution witness. Most of all, I wanted to show her the letter. I wanted to scrutinise her face as she read it and hear her justification, if indeed she had any. Now, I would never have closure and it was a pill so bitter I could not swallow it. It jammed in my throat, choking me.

Mum's death, and the timing of it, seemed to symbolise our whole relationship; there were more questions than answers, and so much left unsaid.

Chapter Thirty

A FEW days after Mum's death, I was on my way back from working in Newcastle when the police called. I was now working for a rail company, as a site project administrator, responsible for health and safety. I enjoyed my job, but it was demanding, with a lot of travelling. The officer explained I was required to make a further witness statement, to satisfy certain questions raised by the defence.

"Can you do the interview this week?" the officer asked.

"Not really," I replied. "I'm busy at work, I'm under a lot of stress, and my Mum has just passed away. I have to arrange her funeral. I really don't see what the rush is, I've heard nothing for months."

He told me the defence had also requested copies of my mobile phone records, which I flatly refused to share.

"They're of no relevance to the trial," I said. "None at all. If I hand over my phone, I'll have to tell my bosses at work, because I use my phone for my job. I don't want people at work to know all about the trial. Really, I just can't cope with any more embarrassment or upset."

Already, due to regular routine drug testing at work, I'd had to confide in my boss why I was taking medication, including anti-depressants. No matter what anyone said, there was a stigma and a shame attached. I did not want, professionally, to be forced to share anything else. And in truth, I just didn't see why the defence teams were allowed to make random demands, when my own requests went largely ignored. I was cornered in my own home, afraid to walk to the local shops, terrified even to look at myself in a mirror, whilst my father and Stephen were free to roam up and down the country. It just wasn't fair.

The more I brooded, the more I resented the idea. I felt the police investigation was intruding on my grief. But all that week, I felt under pressure to make a second statement.

"I just don't feel up to it," I fretted. "I won't be able to concentrate. I have to give priority to my mother's funeral. It doesn't feel right to give a police interview when my mother has only just died."

"Maybe we can work around the funeral," the officer suggested.

"No," I snapped. "The funeral comes first."

I was aware I was being touchy, but the words left my mouth before I could stop them. I felt everyone was against me. I didn't trust anyone, including the police. It was a legacy of the abuse. My life had been shaped by my role as a victim and I was wary even of the people who wanted to help me. Again, I asked myself what kind of woman I might have been, without this trauma.

In the end, I had no choice but to agree to make a statement the day after the funeral. Again, as with my birthdays, I felt every aspect of my life was being invaded. I was not allowed to celebrate, or to grieve, without the abuse rearing its ugly head. In Pembrokeshire, I visited Mum at the funeral parlour to say my final goodbye.

"What did you know?" I asked her sadly. "What were you hiding from me?"

I wanted so much to forgive her, but I didn't really know what I was forgiving her for. I didn't blame her for what she had done. But I resented what she hadn't done.

"I love you, Mum," I whispered, eventually.

As I walked outside, into a biting winter wind, my mind was clouded with confusion and sadness. At her funeral, later that same week, I wrote and read a poem:

The pain I feel today will fade
The pain I feel tomorrow will pass
The guilt I feel will always be there
Secrets have now died, will always haunt me.

* * * *

I was still in a daze, following Mum's funeral, when I made a second police statement. Afterwards, I regretted it. I wasn't in the right frame of mind at all. And as Darren and I drove back home to South Yorkshire, I barely said a word. I felt so flat and numb, like a scrap of paper, like a piece of litter in the street. Once more I was overwhelmed with a desire to escape this miserable world. In the next minute, I was awash with guilt for wanting to leave my daughters and Darren behind. In turn, the guilt triggered feelings of self-loathing and self-blame, and I became suicidal again. I just could not escape this cycle. Again, Darren stepped in as my saviour. Eager to distract me, he showed me a photo on his phone of eight beautiful German Shepherd puppies, advertised by a breeder in Nottingham.

"Would you like one?" he asked.

"Oh yes," I squealed. "Yes please!"

We had been refunded the money from our original wedding booking, and there seemed no better way to spend it.

That weekend we drove to Nottingham. All the puppies were so cute, I just couldn't choose. But then, as I sat back, one small puppy trotted over to me and laid her head on my foot.

"This is the one," I beamed.

We took her home with us that same day, aged 12 weeks, and named her Kayla. I think Darren had intended for me to look after her, as a diversion. But as time went on, Kayla began looking after me too! She grew into such a clever dog, sensing instinctively when I was especially stressed or upset. She would follow me in and out of every room, never letting me out of her sight. Some days, I just didn't want to leave the house, but Kayla would stand patiently by the door and quietly insist I took her out. I felt safe with her. She reminded me so much of Fire, and never since my beloved horse had I felt such a connection with an animal. Like him, she became my best pal and my anchor, my safe haven in a storm.

I thought of Fire often, even now. I would never know

his final fate but in my mind, his handsome face and his cute rollovers lived on. One evening, in February 2022, Darren came home from working with the veterans' charity, brimming with excitement.

"I got called in to see the big boss today," he said. "He told me he might have some exciting news for us soon, but he can't confirm it yet."

We were both equally puzzled. A few days later, after another session helping at the charity, Darren burst through the door, waving a white envelope.

"Guess where we're going?" he asked. "Buckingham Palace!"

I read the letter and learned that through the charity, we'd been invited to a palace garden party.

"Wow!" I grinned. "It's amazing."

My next thought was of Nan and Grandad and their own trip to the palace. History was repeating itself.

"I wish Nan was here, she'd be so proud," I said wistfully.

It felt to me that she was orchestrating this whole event, having a hand in the invites and sending me a little pick-me-up, just when I needed it most. The garden party gave me the perfect excuse to go out shopping and buy myself a new dress. And it took my mind off the trial, at least for a little while, which was scheduled, at last, for the following month, March 2022.

* * * *

Time had dragged during the investigation, but with a trial

date in place the weeks slipped by so quickly it felt as if they were running away from me, and I couldn't keep pace. I stopped eating again, too. Partly, it was a physical problem. I found I could not actually chew, and I had no appetite at all. But the root of it was psychological and buried deep within my soul. The voice told me I did not deserve to eat.

You let him do it, she reminded me, her ghostly tone detached and mocking. *You let him do it, and now, you must be punished.*

I fought against her, forcing a sandwich into my mouth. I needed my strength for the trial, and mentally I had to be alert. But my chest fluttered with panic each time I envisaged going to court. My mouth dried up, making it impossible for me to swallow.

Already slim, in the weeks before the case began, I lost a stone in weight. Shortly before the start date, I was told I would not be required at the court building in Swansea, since Covid restrictions in Wales remained stricter than those in England. I would instead be giving evidence over live-stream, from Sheffield Crown Court. I was doubtful whether this was preferable, but it seemed I didn't have a choice.

The trial was listed to last for three weeks, and I was advised to book three days off work, to give my evidence. But a couple of days beforehand, the trial schedule changed and my dates off work had to be altered. By now, it was too late for me to rearrange my diary, and I was forced into taking unpaid leave. Again, that swell of resentment. Why was it always me conceding and accommodating? It felt that my rights, as a victim, didn't really matter.

Arriving at Sheffield Crown Court, clutching Darren's

hand, my insides were tightly knotted. Facing a rapist in a courtroom is daunting for the strongest individual. But when those rapists are members of your own family, and the rapes are multiple, spanning your entire childhood, the task feels absolutely insurmountable.

As we waited to check in at the main desk, the sound of my chattering teeth reverberated through my head. I was so scared. I remembered poor Bugsy, frightened to death by a passing fox. Could the same happen to me, right here, in the courthouse? Might I drop dead, ironically, before my father had a chance to shoot me? But, as Darren squeezed my hand, I also felt strangely determined. Ever since I was a small girl, I had held onto a ribbon of hope that one day, my voice would be heard. That ribbon had stretched and frayed and at times it had almost snapped. But still, I held it with both hands, and I could not believe that day was finally here.

Naively, something in me still clung to the possibility that my father and Stephen would plead guilty at the last moment.

"I'm afraid not," the usher informed me, as we walked into the witness care room. "They're both pleading not guilty."

It was, in truth, no surprise. They had lied all their lives and so it made little sense for them to stop now. But it stung all the same. Darren and I took our places at a desk, with a live-stream flickering into focus on a screen in front of me. All at once I was teleported back to my bedroom, watching fuzzy *Tom and Jerry* cartoons on my imaginary screen whilst my father assaulted me.

"I can't do it," I whispered.

"You can," Darren whispered back. "I'm here. You can."

On the screen, I could only see the judge and the barristers. But I knew *they* were there. The evil crackled through the ether and seeped out of the edges of my screen. In my mind, I could see those eyes, two black holes, two bottomless pits. I wanted to throw myself in and be buried alive. Anything else, but this. Anywhere else, but here. Gasping, I felt myself collapsing inwards. I could not credit how, on the outside, I was still sitting upright.

"Take your time," the judge said. "If you need to pause at any time, then that's OK."

Uncertainly, I nodded, a large stone in my throat preventing me from replying. But then, the barrister's face loomed into view and the questions began: How old was I? What was I wearing? Who else was there? What was the room like? Why didn't I tell anyone? Why did nobody hear it? The defence teams knew, already, from my witness statements, that I did not have this level of detail, yet they pressed me, over and over, as if hammering in nails. Each time, I felt smaller and smaller. Completely diminished. Bang, bang, bang, the questions were like gunfire. I had a momentary glimpse of my father's guns, lying in his office, waiting to be fired.

"I will shoot you. I will shoot you all."

Because of the live feed, there was a slight time delay, and often the barrister would speak over me, just as I was trying to formulate my response.

"Do you want to answer?" he asked me. "Do you have anything to say?"

"I was told I could take my time," I mumbled. "I'm trying to think about it."

"Hmm," was all he said, and to me, that one single syllable was loaded with judgement and suspicion. I felt he didn't believe me. Again I had that uncomfortable conviction that everyone – the police, the barristers, the judge – were all working against me.

There was a pre-prepared bundle of evidence, handed out to the jury and the legal teams, but I didn't have a copy, since I was giving evidence remotely. I was shown black and white photos of exhibits on the livestream, but they were blurred and indistinct.

"I can't see this clearly," I stuttered, more and more flustered. "I'm sorry, I can't remember this room. I can't answer this question."

"Hmm," the barrister said again. "I see. Hmm."

I felt like he was doubting me, patronising me, questioning my character. Wildly, I looked around, hoping someone would step in to help me. But nobody else seemed to notice. *I am not the liar here!* I wanted to scream.

But instead, I bowed my head, and I was silent. I had no energy or confidence to complain, and what was the point? These people were not on my side. By the time the court finished for the day, I was worn out and weary. Furious at the way I had been challenged, but too exhausted and weak to verbalise it.

"I know the barristers seem harsh, but they're just doing their job," Darren said.

I sighed. I knew he was right. I was taking it all too much to heart. But the second day, after a sleepless night, was even worse.

"So can you describe the layout of the bedroom?" the barrister asked.

"I don't know," I said tearfully. "I'm getting mixed up now. So many different houses."

"Hmm," he replied. "Hmm."

As I got more frazzled and upset, I began coughing, and by the afternoon, my throat was so raw, I was spitting blood into a tissue. After one particularly violent coughing fit, I vomited all down myself.

"We'll take a break," said the judge. "So that you can get medical attention."

The court staff offered to call a doctor, but I knew my cough was triggered purely by stress. There was nothing a doctor could do to help me. I sponged my clothes in the ladies' toilets and had a drink of water. But the prospect of returning to the witness room filled me with dread.

"'I can't go back in there," I told Darren, my voice cracking.

"You can," he said firmly. "You've done so well and you're nearly there now. You cannot let them get away with this. They need to be punished, Sarah. Do this for yourself. Please."

I knew he was right. Yet it took every ounce of courage I could find to take my place again in that chair and submit myself to more humiliation.

Hmm Hmm Hmm…

Each time he said it, he eroded my confidence a little more. I felt he didn't believe a word I said. In one line of questioning, the barrister claimed my father had sent birthday cards and gifts for me, every year, after my parents had separated.

It was not, by any means, my father's biggest lie. But it was such an outrageous claim and seemed to me to epitomise the obscene arrogance which had carried him through his life.

"That just isn't true," I protested. "He never sent a thing. He was never in any way a father figure to me. I met the postman most mornings. I would certainly remember if my Dad had sent me a birthday card. I bet he doesn't even know my date of birth! Ask him!"

"Hmm," said the barrister, and again, I felt it was me, not them, on trial.

After two full days of evidence, my job was done. But I had mixed feelings as I left Sheffield Crown Court. I felt the police and barristers had focussed purely on the letter, because it offered proof of the first attack. The later attacks seemed less significant and dates and places and details which were already sketchy, had become confused in my evidence. I began to worry he might get away with it as he had done for so long.

For the remainder of the trial, I was on eggshells. I continued going to work, determined to follow a routine and also anxious not to take any more time off. Kayla picked up on my worries, and at home, she remained glued to my side. When the jury finally came back, the court staff hastily scrambled a live feed to Swansea Crown Court, and just in time, I managed to tune in for the verdicts. In my mind, I had pictured a grandstand moment, a single cry of 'Guilty!' as my father and brother were led away in handcuffs. In reality, the process was slow and painstaking, and very unclear.

There were so many counts of rape and sexual assault,

some returned guilty verdicts, others did not. Stephen was found guilty of raping me twice. Thanks to the letter, my father was found guilty of raping me, aged three, in the blue bedroom. He was also convicted of multiple rapes and sexual assaults against me. He was found not guilty of several other attacks. This was frustrating, but it was not unexpected. The police had leaned too heavily on the letter in my opinion. And under cross-examination, I had struggled to make myself understood, too. My nerves had got the better of me many times. But afterwards, as Darren and I shared a bottle of wine, he said:

"Sarah, please just be proud of yourself. They're both going to prison for a long time. They'll be off the streets, unable to abuse anyone else. You did it. Let's celebrate."

As we clinked glasses, the relief flowed through me like honey. I sat back, and I allowed his words to sink in.

"They'll be off the streets, unable to abuse anyone else."

And yes, at last I felt proud. I felt clean. I felt heard.

Chapter Thirty-One

QUITE INCREDIBLY, after the verdicts, my father and Stephen were granted bail until sentencing, which had been set for May 27, seven weeks into the future.

"There is no way my father should have been given bail!" I gasped. "What if he comes for me?"

The police reassured me I was safe. But I did not feel it. I was consumed with anxiety, constantly on high alert. Even taking Kayla out walking, one of my favourite daily tasks, was now fraught. I felt I was putting her in danger. What if he shot us both? And the bail conditions seemed to be just another example of my father getting his own way again. He had charmed his way through life, brainwashing his customers, his relatives and his neighbours. And now, he'd manipulated the courts too.

"It's a huge mistake," I told the police. "His rights have come before mine. Yet again."

Luckily, as the weather warmed up and the trees blossomed, I had the perfect diversion as my thoughts turned to the garden party at Buckingham palace. Two weeks before the sentencing, I found myself on a train to London, gazing at the passing blur of fields and towns. Once again, I felt as though I had been sliced right down the middle. One Sarah was left at home, traumatised and broken as she awaited the sentencing of her father and brother. Another Sarah was on her way to Buckingham Palace, with a posh dress and fancy hat in her suitcase and a face full of smiles.

"You OK, love?" Darren asked.

I nodded and squeezed his hand, but could not help thinking of my seven-year-old self; one little girl left at home to be raped by her father, whilst the other skipped off to school. My two lives now, as then, could not be further apart and the contrast was striking and distressing. What I feared most was not one life, or the other – it was falling into the bottomless void that existed between the two. It was this numbing abyss which terrified me more than anything. We arrived at our hotel, unpacked, and spent the remainder of the day wandering around the capital in drizzly weather under an umbrella.

"I hope the rain's going to stop for the garden party tomorrow," I said.

And, luckily, the next morning dawned bright and warm. Again, it felt like another message from Nan, a gift from beyond the clouds. I got changed into my new navy dress with matching jacket, handbag and fascinator. Darren wore his wedding suit, and I helped pin his medals onto his front pocket. As we walked down The Mall, towards the palace, I felt a flutter of excitement.

"I can't believe we're actually going in there!" I squealed. "Remember when we stood outside, and you offered to take me in for a brew, to meet your boss? Now it's happening for real."

"I had it planned, all along," Darren joked.

We stood for a moment at the gates, to take in the scene, and a familiar-looking man tapped Darren on the arm and said:

"Can I ask about your medals? I can't help noticing you've got quite a collection."

He and Darren chatted for a few minutes as I racked my brains as to how I recognised him. It was only after we had said goodbye, and I was walking away, that I shrieked:

"That was Wayne Sleep! The famous dancer!"

I turned around to see him laughing.

"That's right," he confirmed.

"Oh, you wouldn't want to see me dance," Darren told him. "I have two left feet."

"Listen, I can teach anyone to dance," Wayne replied with a smile.

Once inside the palace, we were met with a conveyor belt of celebrities; I spotted Anita Harris, Tony Blackburn and members of the casts of *Strictly Come Dancing* and *Gogglebox*.

"This is surreal," I whispered to Darren.

We walked around the beautiful palace grounds in the spring sunshine as a band played in the background. And later, in the queue for miniature sandwiches and cakes, I found myself next to the TV star, Su Pollard.

"I hope you don't mind me saying, I loved *Hi-de-Hi!*," I told her.

She thanked me and hugged me, and to my delight, she

was just as funny and chatty as her character in the show. As we picked out canapes together, I felt as though I had made a new friend. When the afternoon drew to a close, I spotted a familiar face from the army dinners which Darren and I had attended.

"Hello!" I called, waving merrily. "Remember me?"

"Do you know who that is?" Darren asked, stifling a giggle. "It's Lord Dannatt."

I clapped my hand over my mouth in alarm, but luckily Lord Dannatt was smiling back.

"Look who's standing next to him," Darren whispered, nudging me. "Are you going to shout hello to her, too?"

To my astonishment, Princess Anne was just a couple of metres away, deep in conversation with Lord Dannatt.

"Oh no," I blushed. "I can't do that. I just can't."

I was too shy even to smile at her. But as we made our way back to the tube station, I felt myself glowing fondly at the memory of the day. And I realised I hadn't thought once about my father or my brother, or the sentencing. For those few hours I had forgotten about the other Sarah completely. Once more, I remembered Nan, my own Queen, in her palace in the sky. And I felt sure she had engineered this small pearl of happiness, just for me.

"Thanks Nan," I whispered. "I had such a great day. It was exactly what I needed."

Chapter Thirty-Two

TWO WEEKS on, my father and brother were due to be sentenced. I had written my own impact statement and had requested to read it myself, in court.

It was a journey of over four hours from our home and so Darren suggested we take our touring caravan, stopping off on the way back.

"We could book onto a caravan site for a few days after it's over," he said.

I nodded. We'd both be ready for a break by then.

The journey down ached with silence, Darren did his best to make conversation, but I was too uptight even to think of replies. We found a parking place for the caravan, before making our way into Swansea Crown Court. We waited in a small, windowless side room, and I read and reread my statement, so often I almost knew it by heart. But the time for the sentencing came and went and we were not called into court. We had no idea what was happening.

"There seems to be some delay," our barrister explained. "We'll find out more in due course."

He went off to talk to the judge and when he returned, he revealed my father had failed to show in court. My mind returned immediately to the decision to let him out on bail. I knew the type of liar he was. I had known it was a mistake. My father's wife informed the police she had dropped him at the railway station, with the understanding he was taking the train to Swansea to be sentenced. Officers were dispatched to the train station to check the CCTV but found he had failed to leave the train – if indeed he was ever on it.

Meanwhile, Darren and me were stuck in the airless witness room, hour after hour. With every minute that ticked by, my unease seemed to rise a notch. I was bristling all over with stress. By 4.30pm, I had had enough. I poked my head out, into the corridor and said:

"Do you know what time we'll be going into court please?"

"Oh, the hearing finished some time ago," an usher told me.

My anxiety suddenly mutated into anger. Once again, as the victim, I felt like I was at the very bottom of the list of priorities. I had made the long trip here, Darren and I had both taken time off work and I hadn't slept for days in preparation. And it was all for nothing. Nobody had even had the decency to let me know. Later, when I managed to speak to the barrister, he explained the judge had not wanted to sentence Stephen on his own and so had adjourned the hearing.

"Why was I not told?" I demanded. "I had asked to be in court. Why was I not there?"

But whilst I was seething, the barrister informed me my

father had absconded and could not be found. He was officially on the run and there was a warrant out for his arrest. With that, my annoyance quickly turned to fear.

"What if he comes for me?" I gasped. "Maybe he didn't show today because he's planning something. Maybe he's going to kill me, at long last. This is it."

Images of the guns rattled across my eyeline, and I clung to Darren to steady myself.

"Try not to worry," he told me. "He has no idea where you are."

We had booked in at a small caravan site, but I could not settle at all. Every time I heard a car engine, or a voice outside, I went into spasms of panic, convinced he was coming for me. I felt his hand over my mouth, just as if it was happening all over again. I smelled the cigars. I heard the malign, metallic, clink of his belt. As the first pink streaks of dawn appeared in the sky, I wondered, wearily, whether I would ever be free of my father.

Two days on, I learned he had been arrested and taken into custody. He had told the police he had taken the wrong train, ended up in Bristol, got into a fight at the train station and fallen into the harbour and got wet. It was a ridiculous pack of lies and nobody believed him. The following month, Darren and I made the journey once again to Swansea Crown Court and this time, Lolly wanted to come too. I was again determined to read out my own statement in court, and to face my father and brother.

"I don't want screens or any kind of protection, thank you," I told the usher. "I want to look at them both."

My skin was shrinking with pure terror as I made my way into the courtroom.

My father and my older brother were brought in, flanked by officers, and my stomach flipped over. Stephen looked unwell, his head drooping, as though he felt sorry for himself. My father stared at me, and this time, I was ready for him. I stared straight back, and held his gaze, just for a moment. Deep in my core, something shuddered as those black eyes fixed on mine. The depravity radiated from him, like heat. There was no remorse or regret. Not a shred of mercy or compassion. I remembered the way those eyes had glinted in the darkness, bottomless black pools, dragging me in and forcing me under. Well, not anymore. Today was my day. I pulled my gaze away and focussed on my statement. When I was called to speak, I cleared my throat and turned to the judge.

"I have come to court today so that I can take back control of my life," I said. "They had that control over me for over 50 years… People say once punishment has been given I can move on with my life. It's impossible to move on from the trauma of rape. Rape, assault and mental manipulation that they put me through is a life sentence. Rape is murder of innocence in a child, that's how I can only describe what they did to me."

I had with me a photo of myself, aged three, taken, I estimated, shortly before the rape.

"I want to show this picture of me at the age of around three years old. I am a happy, smiling little girl," I said sadly. "This photo was taken before the heinous act of my first vicious assault."

The Letter

Staring at the photo, I could barely believe it was me. Again, I felt entirely separate and estranged from her; as though the other Sarah, the abused Sarah, had been amputated from me. But I steered my mind back to my statement and continued to read.

"How could a father do that to their own child? Those injuries of pain and suffering will haunt me for the rest of my life... I have continuous flashbacks, nightmares, the intrusive images of the horror and pain I've suffered. I have the feelings of suffocation... Bill and Stephen stole my childhood... I will never get my childhood back."

The court was told that Arthur William Bowditch, 74, and Arthur Stephen Bowditch, 54, had been convicted of multiple counts of rape and indecent assaults against young girls, of whom one was me. The court heard Bowditch junior had a previous conviction from 1989 for indecent assaults of a girl under 14. This was another bombshell. I had no idea Stephen had a criminal record. I worked out his conviction would have been around the time I gave birth to Lolly, and he had visited us whilst she was a baby. The realisation curdled inside my stomach. It was yet another shameful family secret. I could only hope there were no more lurking around us.

Judge Huw Rees said the defendants' victims had been "denied a childhood" by their actions and said the statements from the victims had been "harrowing" to hear. He said it was clear the abuse inflicted by the defendants had profoundly affected all victims. The judge added that my father had acted out of "degenerate and unhealthy sexual lust".

My father was given a 21-year extended sentence, comprising 20 years in custody followed by a one-year extended licence. Stephen was sentenced to 12 years in prison. Both were informed they would be registered sex offenders for the rest of their lives.

****

Oddly, I felt limited satisfaction, or little emotion at all, following the sentencing. It made little difference to me how long my father and Stephen spent in prison. I had hoped, more than anything, that they would admit their guilt. When that didn't happen, I had wanted only for my voice to be heard and believed. Even so, I was relieved they were locked up, away from other young girls. I knew society would be a safer place without them. After the conclusion of the trial, I was awarded compensation from the Criminal Injuries Compensation Authority. But again, the payment brought me little pleasure.

With this colossal chapter behind me, I returned immediately to work, believing, as always, I could distract myself by keeping busy. But there were so many loose ends crowding my mind, and each time I pulled at a strand, it unravelled into another problem.

I was unhappy with the way the police had handled my case and I requested a meeting with the officers. I didn't want to complain or criticise any individuals, but I did want the force to learn and make changes that could be implemented in future investigations. However, despite my attempts to set the meeting up, it never happened. I was also tormented by aspects of the prosecution that had focussed on my family background and my education. I needed to see those facts for myself, because it was vital there were no more secrets, no more landmines waiting to explode. And so I requested copies of my social services records. A fat bundle of papers quickly landed, and they made miserable reading. The records confirmed my spells in and out of foster care as a toddler. In one report, I was described as: *a rather small two-year-old, but looks bright as a button with her rosy cheeks and shining eyes…*

My heart ached when I thought of how those rosy cheeks and shining eyes had been so brutally scratched out. One year after this, I had been raped.

It seemed some of the foster placements had been arranged privately and there were complaints in the records of my father failing to pay the foster parents. I found the newspaper cutting, too, which related to my mother's account of her running away after my father had attacked her. The headline: *Mother of Two is Missing* left me cold. The article said Mrs Florence Bowditch, aged 23, had disappeared from her home and that police and her husband were anxious to trace her. My father was quoted:

"I think there has been some misunderstanding."

"That's some understatement," I said grimly.

Looking further through the records, I found papers which confirmed I had been in foster care on my second birthday. This wasn't a revelation, I had known this for some time, but it broke my heart all over again.

In the weeks afterwards, I realised reading my social services records had brought me no closure, only more heartache. I needed to read my records. I needed to face my father and brother in court. I needed to relive the abuse. But I was beginning to fear this need would eventually kill me. I had always suffered from broken sleep and bad dreams, but now they had become horrific. In nightmares, I had vivid flashbacks to the abuse, where I could clearly feel my father's clammy hand across my mouth and his scratchy beard grazing my cheek. Even in my dreams, I could smell the stale cigars and the sickly scent of Nivea. When I woke, I was gagging on the stench.

"Sarah, are you OK?" Darren asked, sitting up in bed beside me. "You were shouting out in your sleep."

Even though I was awake, I was back there still. His hand was over my mouth, and I felt suffocated, pinned down, as though he was trying to stop me breathing.

"Deep breaths," Darren said gently. "Nice and slowly."

Kayla, who had been sleeping at the bottom of our bed, uncurled herself and came to lie next to me, so that her body was pressed against mine, warm and soft.

"She always knows when you're upset," Darren smiled.

And though I welcomed her affection, my mind flashed back to Fire and the way he would pucker up for a kiss when he sensed I was sad.

There had been so much suffering and I felt smothered by it. Throughout the second part of 2022, I tried many remedies to improve my sleep patterns, hot baths, herbal teas and meditation. I was prescribed sleeping medication, too. But my nightmares just got worse. In one recurring dream, I was plunged back to the day I had said no to my father, and he had pulled me off the back of the sofa by my hair. In my nightmare, he had his hands around my throat, squeezing, squeezing, harder still. On one level, I was aware I was dreaming. But when I woke, sweating and rigid with fear, my throat felt swollen and sore. It was as if reality and dreamland had become enmeshed, and I could no longer distinguish between the two.

In those dark and lonely hours, whilst Darren and Kayla slept, it was neither day nor night. And I was neither alive nor dead. And in truth, waking was not the relief you might imagine it to be, often it was accompanied by a soul-crushing disappointment. For a part of me still wanted to die. A part of me wished he had continued squeezing. And with that confession, I was swamped by guilt; how could I wish I was dead when I had my daughters, Darren and Kayla to think of? It was selfish and self-centred. Yet still, I wished I was dead. On those difficult days, when morning finally came, I could not bring myself to leave the bedroom. I was too scared even to pull the duvet back. I was not scared of death, I was scared of something much worse. A nameless, formless fear. A haunting. Cornered in my bedroom, like a frightened animal, I was too disorientated even to brush my teeth or take a shower. Patiently, Darren squeezed the toothpaste onto my toothbrush and handed it to me.

"Here," he said. "Clean your teeth. You'll feel so much better."

But an hour later, I was still leaning over the sink, with the toothbrush in my hand. I did not have the energy to clean my own teeth. Another day, I managed, with difficulty, to get myself into the shower. But when I emerged, my hair was foamy and full of soap, I had forgotten to rinse the conditioner.

"I can't even look after myself, it's basic hygiene," I sobbed. "What's happening to me?"

Other mornings, I would stand for ages in the shower, with the dial on the hottest setting. I forced myself to stand under the scalding stream of water, gritting my teeth as my skin burned red and raw.

"You deserve this," I told myself. "You're not clean."

On the mornings when I risked going downstairs, I was bombarded with triggers for my trauma. Not only was my home under threat, but it also became a threat in itself. I could not slice a loaf of bread because the sharp knife filled with me an overwhelming desire to harm myself. And even if I overcame this, I was engulfed with flashbacks and memories, so harsh and vivid, it felt as if my father's presence was in my kitchen. Even as I boiled the kettle, I felt his hand clamped over my mouth. I smelled that sickly mix of sweat and cigars. Like a fox, I sniffed the air and I sensed he was nearby.

On occasion, I tried to cook dinner, but it always ended in disaster. Once, I left a pan on until it boiled dry. Another time, I set sausages on fire under the grill. Each time, Darren stepped in to save me. He locked away the sharp knives and all my medication and he took over the cooking and household tasks.

"Don't worry," he said. "We'll get you through this."

But I could not fail to see the worry on his face; this was so hard for him, too. I felt guilty that I was making him suffer, guilty that I had brought this pain into our home, guilty that I had let myself be abused. Even now – with a guilty verdict and my abusers behind bars – a small, insistent, part of me blamed myself.

I was signed off work due to my health, and again, I felt a crippling sense of failure. Darren, too, had to take time off work, to help look after me. On the days when he had to work, I forced myself to take Kayla out of the house. But it felt as if my environment was deliberately placing temptation in my path, throwing down the gauntlet to see if I could make it home alive. I had visions of throwing myself in front of a car. When we walked past the railway, I imagined lying down on the tracks. On bridges, I envisaged throwing myself off the top, landing in a broken and useless heap below. The intrusive thoughts became increasingly vivid and persuasive, and my hands itched to climb the bridge, my feet pulled me towards the road. But each time, as if she could read my mind, Kayla gently but firmly nuzzled me back to safety, away from the railway, back from the bridge, onto the pavement.

Let's get you home, she seemed to say. *I want you where I can keep an eye on you.*

If it hadn't been for her, there were many days when I simply would not have made it home alive. It was as if the trial – and the recollection of the abuse – had sparked an irreversible downslide in my health. My box of memories, now unlocked, were spreading like expanding foam, and they couldn't be squashed back in.

I saw a doctor but the mental health waiting lists, again, were long. As with the barristers, and the police, I was not sure the medical profession was on my side. I was not sure there was anyone on my side – even myself. Especially myself.

Meanwhile my dreams became even worse. In one nightmare, which recurred frequently, Dad shot me through the driver's window of my car. I had stopped driving, because of my anxiety, but on this occasion, in my dream, I was back behind the wheel. As I turned to check the traffic, at a junction, he appeared alongside me. He tapped on the window, telling me to open it, and even though I knew what was coming, I did as he said. I always did as he said. In many ways, it was a relief. I had lived in fear of this all my life, I felt I'd been stood in the corner for over 50 years, waiting for him to thrash me with his belt. The anticipation was intolerable. Now, at least, as my window whirred downwards, it was over. Even in my dream, I could actually feel the cool metal of the barrel pressed against my cheek. I heard the click and I saw my own brains splattered across the windscreen, red, pink and slimy white.

Another night, I was ambushed by both of my abusers. Stephen flipping me over expertly and pinning me to the bed. Dad tilting his chin, inclining his head, nailing me to the bed simply with a glare from his black eyes. And the barrister, the cold, clinical barrister, interrupting the clink of Dad's belt with his: "Hmm. Hmm. Hmm." The sound of him humming was almost more frightening than the prospect of the assault. I could not fight them off. I never had, and never would. Instead, I closed my eyes and searched for a dream within a dream – a cartoon or a memory to help me climb out of this nightmare. But then, floating above me, her face purple with fury, was the other Sarah.

Kick them! she yelled. *Punch them! You're not a kid anymore! You went to court, they're in prison. You don't need to stand for this. Not anymore!*

I did my best, kicking and screaming and punching. But I was useless against my father's strength.

"You say a word and I will shoot you."

"You tell anyone, I will say you wanted it."

"Hmm. Hmm. Hmm."

In panic, I woke, with my father's hand over my mouth.

"I can't breathe!" I gasped. "Get him off me!"

But it was Kayla, laying across me, trying to calm me down. Darren, already awake, was standing at the side of the bed, his face creased with concern.

"You're hurting yourself," he said. "Stop thrashing about. What's the matter?"

I didn't know where to start, or how to tell him. But after we clicked on the light, I saw my legs and arms were covered in bruises and pinch marks. I had injured myself, trying to fight back. Perhaps the injuries were from the other Sarah, and it was her way of trying to wake me up, pinching me until the pain snapped me out of my sleep.

These nightmares became alarmingly regular, and I often awoke with bruises. My arms and legs were dotted with purple splodges, and I had no idea whether they were signs of a fight back, or further signs of self-harm. Perhaps they were both.

One of my most disturbing dreams did not even feature my father. I had a nightmare where I would climb into Mum's coffin, to keep her warm. I knew how she hated to be cold, and I couldn't help myself. As I held her close, her body was stiff and unyielding. Even in dreams, she did not return my affection. And I noticed, in alarm, that her icy-cold hand was the exact same hand that had stroked my face at the start of my eating disorder. One and the same. When I awoke, scrabbling to get out of the coffin, I was furious with myself. Why did I always have to put my mother before myself, sacrifice my own life to keep her warm? Even now she was dead, I was still trying to please her. It was as though she was the child, and I was the mother. Our roles, always ill-defined, had been completely reversed.

In the lonely abyss of the early hours, I was suspended in limbo, trapped by my own trauma. Over and over, I called out to my mother, but there was never any reply.

"Why?" I sobbed. "Why did you tell the doctors I fell onto a go-cart? Why did you lie for my father? Why did you refuse to testify in court for me?"

And, even in my nightmares, this question cut right through me, worse than all the others:

"Did you ever love me, Mum?"

The unanswered pleas went on and on. Simultaneously, I loved and loathed her. Again, I was divided down the centre, one Sarah could not mourn her, could not even admit she was dead, she loved her mother and wanted only for her mother to love her back. The other Sarah was desperate to confront her mother and was raging at the way she had been failed. Both Sarahs were riddled with guilt. Both Sarahs were trapped in the past. I felt there was no escape. Regularly, I woke in the night, screaming in terror and with bruises and pinch marks down my arms and legs, physical manifestations of the mental turmoil which raged inside my head.

Chapter Thirty-Three

ONE MORNING in March 2023, one year on from the trial, I woke to a world so alien it felt almost like an outer body experience. Even as I opened my eyes, I was crying uncontrollably. Darren had left for work already and Kayla padded across the bed to lick my tears away. I sensed her concern, but I could not even speak to allay her fears. I was in some sort of fugue-like state, and my old self had been locked away and could not get out.

Most of my life I had been divided into two Sarahs. Now, they had both vanished and there was nothing left in my body, except for a shell. I felt completely empty.

Pulling myself up in bed, my hands felt they no longer belonged to me. I touched my fingers to my face, but my cheeks were numb, the skin a different texture. Kayla lay on the bed beside me, her tail gently swishing against my legs. Slowly – it might have taken minutes or even hours – my tears slowed. And then, it began. Before my eyes, a little like the live-stream from the court, a film of my life started to play. It was as clear and lucid as if it was on a TV screen

The Letter

right in front of me. Slightly fast-forwarded, it began with the first rape in the blue bedroom, and it covered every attack, every rape, every beating – even the ones I didn't know I had stored in my memory bank.

In silent horror, I watched the rapes in the stables and in my bedroom, the assaults in the horsebox, in my father's bedroom and in the bathroom. When it ended, with the two rapes by Stephen at my mother's house, the TV screen was plunged into darkness. Looking into a black nothing was like staring into my father's eyes. The desire to jump in, to bury myself in this deep hole, was irresistible. Disorientated and sad, but firm with purpose, I knew suddenly what was needed. The film was a last goodbye, and this was my cue to leave the world. Alive with an infusion of energy and spirit, I did a quick circuit of the room, looking for the quickest, cleanest solution. The window. Of course. Without a second's hesitation, I ran to the window and flung it open, ready to throw myself out to my death.

But as I climbed onto the sill, a large, warm body knocked into me and sent me tumbling onto the carpet. As I looked up, Kayla was standing right across the window, barring my way.

"Kayla," I whispered, only just aware of her, and of myself. "You saved my life."

When she was satisfied I was calm, she left her post at the window and came to lie with me, on the carpet.

"You saved my life," I told her again, burying my head in her fur.

I did not know if I was happy or sad, relieved or dismayed.

But I was completely in awe of her intelligence and intuition.

When Darren came home from work, she and I were lying on the bedroom carpet together, sleeping. I was exhausted by what I later learned was the beginning of a mental breakdown. I was referred for mental health help and diagnosed with PTSD, depression and adjustment reaction disorder. I felt strongly that the trial, and the reemergence of so much buried trauma, had contributed to my breakdown. But I also knew that my mother's betrayals, and subsequent death, had played their part, too.

I could find no resolution for my heartbreak. Days after my suicide attempt at the bedroom window, I was seized by a compulsion to do it again. This time, unable to cope with the flashbacks which scuttled across my eyeline like cockroaches, I ran into the bathroom. I forced open the locked cabinet where my medication was kept and crammed as much as I could into my mouth. As I swallowed the first few pills, I felt only relief. But I had not reckoned on Kayla, my best friend, my protector and my therapist. She ran into the bathroom, barking loudly, before dashing downstairs to alert Darren.

"Sarah, no!" he exclaimed, grabbing the tablets from my hand. "This isn't the right way, love."

Together, he and Kayla surrounded me with a hug. If it was possible to cure me with love alone, then my recovery would have been instant. In the depths of my despair were pockets of real hope. And gratitude too. I was so lucky to have a wonderful husband and a wonderful dog.

The Letter

****

My suicide attempts continued, alarming and erratic, and I felt as though I had no control over whether I lived or died. Everything around me would suddenly go black – the black of my father's eyes – and I was helpless to resist the compulsion to hurt myself.

Once, out with Elesha, my stepdaughter, I tried to throw myself in front of a moving car. Thankfully, her quick reactions saved my life. Another time, out for a couple of drinks at my friend's pub, I tried to hang myself, with my own belt, in the ladies' toilets. Darren came to my rescue, but I was already unconscious and had to be taken to hospital. Most nights, before I fell asleep, my final thought was: "Please don't let me wake up. Please let this trauma end."

In 2024, I finally began meaningful psychotherapy and counselling to address the issues which had festered for so long in my mind. In addition to coping with the abuse, the trial, and the aftermath, I also had to come to terms with the loss of my mother, and with that, the loss of any redemption and closure. I began to grieve not only for her but also for the answers and the justice I would now never have.

The hardest thing for me, from all of this, is to accept that she has gone, and she has taken her secrets with her. Sometimes, still, my days look bleached of colour, other times, they are blood red. It's up to me, as the artist, to choose my own colours and to paint them back in. I'm not back at work yet, but I spend my time producing 'diamond art', making pictures from precious gems. I've completed several pieces to be auctioned for Help 4 Homeless Veterans. I've even taken on a couple of commissions, too. Now, as when I was small, art brings me so much peace and pleasure.

I've been thinking about taking up horse-riding again, another jigsaw piece from my childhood. Though I am trying to move on, as a whole person, a part of me is still stuck in my early teens, alone and scared. The other Sarah is trapped in the horror house, begging to be released. I hope one day I can be brave enough to return there, to fling open the doors and set her free. Maybe I need to confront my past and face my trauma head on, back where it all began.

I'd also like to visit Bill and Stephen in prison. They no longer have the familial titles of father and brother, they don't deserve them. But I would welcome the chance to face them and hear them admit what they did. Those words would mean more to me than any jail sentence. I've been told I probably can't meet them, because of the restraining order which was made after the trial. It's for my own safety, I've been told, yet I do want to visit them. Again, to me, it seems like the victim's voice really isn't being heard.

After the trial, I was invited to appear on an online forum, to try to change police policy and procedure going forwards, in sexual abuse cases. I jumped at the chance. I have so many ideas about how I'd like to change the system for others. I don't believe victims should be referred to as witnesses, we didn't witness the trauma, we experienced it. That's a big difference. I'd recommend having one point of contact within the police. There are too many signposts to witness care, victim liaison and victim support. Victims fall down the cracks and end up getting no help at all. I spoke to other victims on the forum and they, like me, felt forgotten.

I'd also advise earlier involvement of the CPS in cases because fewer mistakes will be made with clearer cross-communication. I believe victims should be kept updated with all the main decisions in the case. Better training is needed for officers working with sex abuse victims, I felt there was a lack of empathy in my case. I'd also recommend a brief 'lessons learned' meeting after a major trial, so police and victims can share their thoughts.

Communication, for me, is key. So far, I've taken part in five forums and I'm waiting to go on a CPS forum later this year. My own experience of the system was not positive, but I hope I can change this for others.

At home, Darren and I are closer and happier than ever. He has taught me the true meaning of love and without him and Kayla, I know I wouldn't be here today. I'm grateful to my daughters, my stepdaughter, and my friends Patsy and Lyndsey. Everyone at Barnsley Sexual Abuse and Rape Crisis Services has been wonderful too.

I hope other abuse victims will realise they should never, ever, feel ashamed. After staying silent for nearly 50 years, it is part of my recovery process to be proud of my survival. All my life, I had no choice, no voice. This is my chance to speak, and I intend to shout loudly. I've had so much pain, but I also have so much to celebrate. I only have to look into Kayla's big brown eyes to know how much I am loved.

For more information, support or advice on any of the issues featured in this book the following organisations may be able to help:

The National Association for People Abused in Childhood
https://napac.org.uk/
Phone: 0808 801 0331
Samaritans
https://www.samaritans.org/
Phone: 116 123
SOS Silence of Suicide
https://sossilenceofsuicide.org/
Phone: 0808 115 1505
BEAT

Providing information and support for anyone affected by an eating disorder.

https://www.beateatingdisorders.org.uk/
Phone: (Eng) 0808 801 0677 (Scot) 0808 801 0432
(Wales) 0808 801 0433 (NI) 0808 801 0434
The National Domestic Abuse Helpline
The 24 hour National Domestic Abuse Helpline, run by Refuge is for women experiencing domestic abuse, their family, friends and others calling on their behalf.
https://www.nationaldahelpline.org.uk/
Phone: 0808 2000 247
The 24/7 Rape & Sexual Abuse Support Line
https://rapecrisis.org.uk/
Phone: 0808 500 2222

Acknowledgements

MY DAUGHTERS and stepdaughter Elesha, my stepfather, my family and friends who continue to inspire me and have helped, not just with my past, but supporting me in getting my voice heard.

To friends who helped myself and Darren get married, I will be eternally grateful.

My best friends Lyndsey, Patsy, Sandra and all the ladies of The Manx Arms Pool team who taught me the true meaning of friendship and those rare, beautiful friendships that change our lives forever. I will always be grateful for the support you all have given.

I dedicate this book to BSCRCS who went above and beyond and supported me throughout the whole investigation. I would not be here today if I did not have your support. Thank you.

To you, dear reader, for making this journey worthwhile, who breathe life into these pages. Thank you for giving my words a chance.

To Ann for the encouragement, the challenges the doubts

and fears and the relentless support in helping me write my one true voice, so that I can encourage others to fight for what's right, help other victims to come forward, so they have a voice and for the women and men who struggle to be heard and get justice.

Finally to Kayla, my lovely German. She is my best friend, my saviour and she knew when I needed her the most. She is my world and now my assistance dog and loveable, fluffy butt pet.

Say goodbye to the past that hunted me
My recovery is now ongoing
My future awaits me with my family
I say, thank you, to you all with love.

Other bestselling Mirror Books written by Ann Cusack